CALM
PARENTING:
A GUIDE TO ANGER MANAGEMENT FOR MOMS AND DADS

Nurturing Harmony in the Midst of Parenthood

Lauren Hayes

© **Copyright 2024 - All rights reserved.**

The content contained within this book may not be reproduced, duplicated or transmitted without direct written permission from the author or the publisher.

Under no circumstances will any blame or legal responsibility be held against the publisher, or author, for any damages, reparation, or monetary loss due to the information contained within this book, either directly or indirectly.

Legal Notice:

This book is copyright protected. It is only for personal use. You cannot amend, distribute, sell, use, quote or paraphrase any part, or the content within this book, without the consent of the author or publisher.

Disclaimer Notice:

Please note the information contained within this document is for educational and entertainment purposes only. All effort has been executed to present accurate, up to date, reliable, complete information. No warranties of any kind are declared or implied. Readers acknowledge that the author is not engaging in the rendering of legal, financial, medical or professional advice. The content within this book has been derived from various sources. Please consult a licensed professional before attempting any techniques outlined in this book.

By reading this document, the reader agrees that under no circumstances is the author responsible for any losses, direct or indirect, that are incurred as a result of the use of information contained within this document, including, but not limited to, errors, omissions, or inaccuracies.

TABLE OF CONTENTS

INTRODUCTION 1

CHAPTER I: Understanding Parental Anger 2
  The Origins of Parental Anger 2
  Impact on Parent-Child Relationships 5
  Breaking the Cycle of Anger 9

CHAPTER II: The Mind-Body Connection 14
  Recognizing Physical and Emotional Triggers 14
  Stress Management Techniques 19
  Mindfulness and Parenting 24

CHAPTER III: Communication Strategies 29
  Effective Listening Skills 29
  Assertive Communication 34
  Teaching Children Emotional Expression 38

CHAPTER IV: Setting Realistic Expectations 43
  Managing Parental Expectations 43
  Age-Appropriate Behavior 47
  Embracing Imperfection 52

CHAPTER V: Anger-Management Techniques for Parents 57
  Deep Breathing and Relaxation Exercises 57

Time-Outs for Parents 62
   Journaling and Reflective Practices 67

CHAPTER VI: Creating a Calm Home Environment 73
   Organizing and Decluttering.. 73
   Designating Relaxation Spaces 78
   Establishing Routines and Boundaries 82

CHAPTER VII: Positive Discipline 88
   Understanding Discipline vs. Punishment............................. 88
   Implementing Positive Reinforcement................................... 94
   Consistency in Parenting 99

CHAPTER VIII: Parental Self-Care 105
   Importance of Self-Care for Parents..................................... 105
   Finding Time for Personal Hobbies...................................... 110
   Seeking Support from Others 115

CHAPTER IX: Parenting as a Team 120
   Effective Co-Parenting Strategies 120
   Communication Between Parents.. 125
   Balancing Responsibilities 130

CHAPTER X: Addressing Specific Parental Challenges 135
   Dealing with Teenage Rebellion 135
   Handling Sibling Conflicts 140
   Navigating Special Parenting Situations
   (e.g., Single Parenting)... 145

CONCLUSION.. 151

INTRODUCTION

Welcome to "Calm Parenting: A Guide to Anger Management for Moms and Dads - Nurturing Harmony amid Parenthood." Parenthood is a rewarding journey filled with love, joy, and growth, but it comes with its share of challenges. As moms and dads navigate the intricate terrain of raising children, managing emotions becomes crucial to fostering a harmonious family environment. This e-book is a comprehensive guide to help parents cultivate calmness and navigate the often-tumultuous waters of anger management.

Being a parent is a life-changing and significant experience marked by moments of triumph and occasional frustration. While the love for our children is boundless, the stressors and demands of parenting can sometimes lead to the expression of anger. Acknowledging and addressing this anger is vital in creating a nurturing and peaceful home for parents and children.

"Calm Parenting" is designed as a supportive resource, offering practical strategies, insights, and exercises to assist moms and dads in understanding, managing, and transforming their anger. We delve into the root causes of parental anger, providing a roadmap for self-reflection and personal growth.

CHAPTER I

Understanding Parental Anger

The Origins of Parental Anger

Parenthood, a profound journey marked by joy, growth, and love, also encompasses many challenges that can evoke strong emotions. Among these emotions, anger often emerges as a powerful force, affecting the parent-child dynamic and family environment. Understanding the origins of parental anger is a critical step in fostering healthy emotional landscapes within families. This section delves into the complex roots of parental outrage, exploring societal influences, personal triggers, and the impact of stressors on the emotional well-being of moms and dads.

At the heart of parental anger lies a confluence of societal expectations, cultural norms, and individual experiences that shape how parents navigate the demanding terrain of raising children. Societal pressure to conform to idealized parenting standards can create an environment where parents feel judged and scrutinized, leading to heightened stress levels. The fear of falling short of these expectations, whether real or perceived, can contribute to feelings of frustration and inadequacy, setting the stage for the emergence of anger as a coping mechanism.

Cultural norms and historical parenting practices also play a significant role in shaping parental anger. In some cultures, there may be implicit expectations regarding parental authority and discipline, which can influence how parents express and perceive anger. Understanding the cultural context is essential in unraveling the complex tapestry of emotions within families, as it allows for a nuanced exploration of how societal and cultural factors contribute to the origins of parental anger.

Individual experiences, including one's upbringing and childhood, profoundly impact how parents navigate parenthood's emotional landscape. Those who experienced harsh discipline or lacked positive role models may find themselves grappling with unresolved emotions that surface as anger when faced with the challenges of parenting. On the other hand, individuals with supportive and nurturing backgrounds may draw from positive experiences, shaping their approach to parenting more constructively. Exploring these personal histories is crucial in understanding how past experiences influence parents' emotional responses.

Modern life's daily stressors and demands contribute significantly to the origins of parental anger. Balancing work responsibilities, financial pressures, and the myriad tasks associated with caregiving can create a high-stress environment for parents. In this context, anger may serve as an emotional release—a reaction to the overwhelming pressure and a manifestation of the struggle to maintain equilibrium in the face of constant demands. Recognizing and addressing these external stressors is pivotal in developing strategies to manage anger effectively.

Parental anger often intersects with the challenges of communication within families. The inability to express emotions openly and constructively can lead to the suppression of anger, which may later resurface in unexpected and intense ways. Conversely, the lack of effective communication channels between parents and children can contribute to misunderstandings, exacerbating parental frustration and anger. Exploring healthy communication patterns and fostering open dialogue within the family is integral to breaking the cycle of rage and creating a more supportive emotional environment.

Moreover, the expectations parents set for themselves can be a significant source of anger when unmet. Striving for perfection or attempting to fulfill unrealistic ideals can lead to self-imposed stress and frustration. Accepting that imperfection is a natural part of the parenting journey and embracing self-compassion allows parents to navigate challenges with a greater sense of resilience and understanding, mitigating the potential for anger to surface.

The role of external influences, such as media portrayals of parenting and societal narratives, should be considered when examining the origins of parental anger. Media often perpetuates unrealistic depictions of idealized parenting, creating unrealistic expectations that contribute to feelings of inadequacy and frustration among parents. Societal narratives that equate anger with assertiveness or control can also influence parental behavior, shaping how parents express and perceive their emotions within the family dynamic.

In conclusion, the origins of parental anger are multifaceted, encompassing societal expectations, cultural influences, personal experiences, and the impact of daily stressors. By unraveling the complex interplay of these factors, parents can gain valuable insights into the roots of their anger, fostering a deeper understanding of their emotional landscape. Recognizing the societal, cultural, and individual dimensions of parental anger allows for a more holistic approach to anger management, empowering parents to navigate the challenges of parenthood with resilience, empathy, and a commitment to fostering a healthier emotional environment within their families.

Impact on Parent-Child Relationships

Parental anger, a complex and often challenging emotion, can profoundly affect the parent-child relationship, shaping family dynamics. Understanding the impact of parental anger on these crucial relationships is essential for fostering healthy emotional connections and promoting a supportive family environment. This section explores the multifaceted repercussions of parental anger on parent-child relationships, delving into the emotional, psychological, and long-term effects that can ripple through the fabric of family life.

At its core, parental anger is a powerful emotional signal within the parent-child relationship. As keen observers of their parents' behavior, children are highly attuned to the nuances of emotional expression. When parents express anger through verbal outbursts or non-verbal cues, children internalize these signals, often interpreting them as indicators of disapproval, rejection, or fear. The impact on the emotional well-being of children can be significant, contributing to feelings of insecurity, anxiety, and a distorted sense of self-worth.

The emotional toll of parental anger extends beyond the immediate reaction to the anger itself. Children may internalize the message that they are the cause of their parents' anger, leading to feelings of guilt or inadequacy. The fear of parental anger can create heightened alertness, inhibiting the child's ability to express themselves openly or take age-appropriate risks. Over time, these emotional responses can shape the child's self-perception and influence their overall emotional resilience.

The psychological impact of parental anger on children is closely tied to the formation of attachment patterns and the development of emotional regulation skills. Secure attachment, characterized by trust and emotional safety, is crucial for healthy child development. However, repeated exposure to parental anger can disrupt the formation of specific attachments, potentially leading to insecure attachment styles. Children may develop anxious or avoidant attachment patterns, influencing their capacity to establish wholesome relationships and deal with emotional difficulties as they age.

Parental anger can also influence the child's emotional regulation skills. Youngsters watch and emulate their parents to learn how to control their emotions. If a parent consistently expresses anger uncontrolled or aggressively, the child may model similar behaviors, leading to challenges in managing their feelings appropriately. This learned response to anger can impact the child's social interactions, academic performance, and overall well-being.

In addition to the immediate emotional and psychological impact, parental anger can shape the long-term trajectory of parent-child relationships. The loss of trust between parents and children is one possible outcome. Trust can be eroded, and a sense of uncertainty can arise when kids perceive their parents' anger as irrational or unexpected. Trust must be rebuilt for the parent-child relations to be repaired and strengthened.

Furthermore, parental anger can significantly influence the dynamics of power and authority within the family. Children may perceive anger as a control tool, leading to compliance out of fear rather than a genuine understanding of consequences. This dynamic can hinder the development of internalized values and self-discipline in children, as they may prioritize avoiding punishment over understanding the rationale behind behavioral expectations. Striking a balance between discipline and open communication is essential for fostering a healthy power dynamic within the parent-child relationship.

The communication patterns within the family are another area profoundly impacted by parental anger. When anger becomes a predominant mode of communication, the exchange of ideas, feelings, and concerns may be stifled. Children may be reluctant to express themselves openly, fearing the potential repercussions of sharing their thoughts or experiences. This communication breakdown can impede the development of a healthy parent-child relationship, as genuine connection relies on open dialogue and mutual understanding.

Parental anger can also influence the formation of coping mechanisms in children. In response to the stress of living in an environment marked by rage, children may develop maladaptive coping strategies such as withdrawal, aggression, or emotional suppression. While initially serving as protective measures, these coping mechanisms can persist into adulthood, affecting the individual's ability to navigate stress and conflict healthily and constructively.

Addressing the impact of parental anger on parent-child relationships requires a multifaceted approach that encompasses self-awareness, communication skills, and a commitment to fostering emotional well-being within the family. Parents can benefit from cultivating mindfulness, which involves being present in the moment and developing a heightened awareness of their emotions and reactions. Mindfulness practices enable parents to respond to situations more calmly and intentionally, reducing the likelihood of expressing anger reactively or impulsively.

Effective communication is a cornerstone of healthy parent-child relationships. Parents may foster an atmosphere that encourages open communication by paying attention to what their children say, acknowledging their emotions, and helping them express their feelings healthily. A sense of security is cultivated in children by setting clear and consistent standards and providing age-appropriate explanations of consequences. This helps youngsters recognize family boundaries.

Seeking professional support, such as family counseling or parenting workshops, can be instrumental in addressing the impact of parental anger on parent-child relationships. Therapeutic interventions provide a safe space for families to explore and navigate the underlying causes of anger, develop effective coping strategies, and strengthen the bonds that form the foundation of healthy family dynamics.

In conclusion, parental anger profoundly impacts parent-child relationships, influencing families' emotional, psychological, and long-term dynamics. Recognizing the ripple effects of parental anger is the first step in fostering a healthy family environment. By prioritizing open communication, cultivating self-awareness, and seeking appropriate support, parents can navigate anger management challenges, fostering a parent-child relationship characterized by trust, emotional resilience, and mutual understanding. In doing so, families can create a nurturing space where children thrive emotionally, psychologically, and in the enduring bonds that shape their lives.

Breaking the Cycle of Anger

Once initiated, the cycle of anger within families can become a persistent and challenging pattern that affects the emotional well-being of all its members. Breaking this cycle requires a deliberate and concerted effort to understand the roots of anger, develop effective coping mechanisms, and foster a nurturing environment that promotes emotional wellness. This section explores the intricate dynamics of breaking the cycle of rage within families, emphasizing the importance of self-awareness and communication and cultivating positive coping strategies to create a healthier and more harmonious family life.

At the core of breaking the cycle of anger lies the recognition that anger is often a symptom of underlying issues, and addressing these issues is paramount to effecting lasting change. Self-awareness becomes crucial in this process, as individuals must introspectively examine their triggers, reactions, and emotional responses. Understanding the source of anger—whether rooted in personal experiences, stressors, or unmet needs—provides the foundation for breaking the cycle and creating a more conscious and intentional approach to emotional expression within the family.

Communication is a linchpin in breaking the cycle of anger, serving as the bridge that connects family members and facilitates understanding. Family members must openly and honestly discuss their emotions, experiences, and concerns. Active listening, empathy, and the capacity for assertive yet polite self-expression are all necessary for effective communication. By creating a safe space for open discourse, families can address underlying issues, dispel misunderstandings, and work collaboratively toward resolving conflicts without resorting to anger as a default response.

Often more vulnerable to parental anger, children benefit significantly from a family environment that prioritizes open communication and emotional expression. As moving guides, parents must teach children healthy ways to express and manage their emotions. By modeling constructive communication and providing a framework for emotional regulation, parents contribute to breaking the cycle of anger and equipping their children with essential life skills for positively navigating emotions.

Breaking the cycle of anger also necessitates cultivating positive coping mechanisms that replace destructive patterns. Rather than relying on anger as an automatic response to stress or frustration, family members can develop alternative strategies such as mindfulness, deep breathing exercises, or engaging in physical activities to channel excess energy. Positive coping mechanisms alleviate the immediate symptoms of anger and contribute to a more resilient and adaptive emotional landscape within the family.

Creating an emotionally safe environment involves fostering a sense of trust, security, and open communication. Parents can achieve this by consistently demonstrating empathy, providing emotional support, and acknowledging their vulnerabilities. Cultivating emotional intelligence within parents sets the stage for an emotionally healthy family dynamic, where anger is addressed proactively rather than perpetuated.

Breaking the cycle of anger is intricately linked to cultivating empathy within the family. Empathy is a potent counterbalance to anger since it entails sharing and comprehending the sentiments of another person. Family members may handle disagreements with empathy and understanding because they know each other's experiences and viewpoints. Family members who put themselves in others' shoes develop a stronger bond and add to a peaceful and encouraging family atmosphere.

Forgiveness plays a pivotal role in breaking the cycle of anger and rebuilding trust within families. Holding onto grudges and resentments perpetuates a cycle of negativity and prevents genuine emotional healing. Family members need to be willing to forgive—both of themselves and other people—and understand that doing so is a purposeful decision to let go of the emotional weight and move on, not to excuse the behaviors that made them angry in the first place. Families can foster development, resilience, and the emergence of healthier relationship patterns by forgiving one another.

Family routines and rituals give the family structure and predictability, which benefits the members' general emotional well-being. A feeling of connection and belonging is cultivated by creating routines for communicating, spending time together, and sharing activities. Without regular rituals, the family could feel more stressed and confused, which raises the possibility that they will become angry in response to problems or disturbances.

In breaking the cycle of anger, seeking external support when needed is crucial. Professional counseling, family therapy, or parenting workshops offer valuable resources for families grappling with persistent anger dynamics. Skilled experts may offer perceptions, instruments, and tactics to deal with the underlying reasons for rage, enhance dialogue, and establish a nurturing atmosphere for every family member. To interrupt harmful patterns and promote positive change, asking for help is a proactive and empowered first step.

Educational initiatives within families contribute significantly to breaking the cycle of anger. By educating family members about the impact of anger on emotional well-being, interpersonal relationships, and overall family dynamics, individuals gain a deeper understanding of the consequences of perpetuating the cycle. Knowledge empowers family members to make informed choices, adopt healthier coping mechanisms, and actively contribute to creating a more emotionally resilient family unit.

In conclusion, breaking the cycle of anger within families is a transformative journey that requires self-awareness, communication, and the cultivation of positive coping mechanisms. Families can replace anger with understanding, empathy, and resilience by addressing the underlying issues contributing to a ger, fostering open communication, and developing healthier ways to manage emotions. Breaking the cycle takes time, effort, and teamwork and a shared commitment to promoting emotional well-being in the family. By making these deliberate efforts, families can break free from anger and provide the groundwork for long-term emotional well-being. They can also pave the way toward a more peaceful and supportive atmosphere.

CHAPTER II

The Mind-Body Connection

Recognizing Physical and Emotional Triggers

The journey to effective anger management begins with the recognition and understanding of both physical and emotional triggers that fuel the flames of anger. Anger is a potent signal in the intricate tapestry of human emotions, warning people of imagined dangers or difficulties. Understanding the complexities of these emotional and physical triggers opens doors to deeper self-awareness. It allows people to react to circumstances intentionally instead of reflexively. This section delves into the subtle aspects of identifying both physical and emotional triggers, highlighting their significance in anger management and fostering mental health in general.

Since physical triggers are often linked to the body's physiological reactions, they are crucial in manifesting wrath. Human nature is shaped by the "fight or flight" response, which results in several physiological reactions such as elevated blood pressure, heart rate, and the creation of stress hormones. These physiological alterations prime the body to respond to perceived dangers. Although evolutionarily adapted, this response may lead to elevated emotional states that encourage an individual's propensity for rage in contemporary situations.

Physical triggers can manifest in various forms, with each person having unique sensitivities to stimuli in their environment. External factors such as loud noises, crowded spaces, or even specific smells can activate the body's stress response, laying the groundwork for anger to emerge. Understanding one's physical triggers involves keen observation and a willingness to identify patterns in the body's reactions to different situations. This awareness provides the foundation for implementing proactive strategies to mitigate the impact of physical triggers on anger.

In addition to external stimuli, internal physical states also contribute to the activation of anger. Factors like fatigue, hunger, or physical discomfort lower the threshold for irritability, making individuals more susceptible to anger. In the hustle and bustle of daily life, individuals may overlook these internal cues, unwittingly allowing physical triggers to accumulate and culminate in rage. Prioritizing self-care, including sufficient rest, nourishment, and regular physical activity, becomes crucial to managing internal physical triggers and promoting overall emotional well-being.

Emotional triggers, intricately linked to thoughts, beliefs, and past experiences, represent another dimension of the anger equation. These triggers are often more complex and sincerely root d, requiring introspection and a willingness to explore the underlying emotional landscape. Understanding emotional triggers involves recognizing patterns of thought and identifying themes that consistently lead to anger. It requires a certain level of vulnerability and co-commitment to delve into the emotional complexities that underlie anger reactions.

Past experiences and unresolved emotions can serve as potent emotional triggers. Traumatic events, feelings of inadequacy, or unmet needs from childhood can resurface in the present, contributing to intense emotional responses, including anger. Acknowledging and processing these deeper emotional triggers often requires the support of therapeutic interventions, such as counseling or psychotherapy, providing individuals with tools to navigate and heal from past wounds.

Cognitive distortions, or patterns of distorted thinking, represent another category of emotional triggers. These distortions, such as black-and-white thinking, catastrophizing, or personalization, can skew one's perception of reality, leading to heightened emotional responses. Recognizing and challenging these distorted thoughts through cognitive-behavioral strategies is instrumental in altering the thought patterns contributing to anger. By cultivating a more balanced and rational perspective, individuals can mitigate the impact of cognitive distortions on their emotional well-being.

Interpersonal relationships, often a source of joy and stress, can be fertile ground for emotional triggers. Unresolved conflicts, unmet expectations, or communication breakdowns can fuel anger within relationships. Recognizing the patterns of interaction and the specific dynamics that trigger anger is essential for fostering healthier relationships. Effective communication, empathy, and active listening become crucial tools in addressing emotional triggers within interpersonal contexts.

The media and societal influences represent external sources of emotional triggers that shape individual perspectives and contribute to anger. Exposure to negative news, societal injustices, or divisive narratives can evoke strong emotional responses. Recognizing the impact of external influences on one's emotional state allows individuals to consume media mindfully, actively choosing sources that align with their values and promoting a more balanced emotional outlook.

Identifying mental and physical triggers requires an ongoing cycle of observation, introspection, and modification. Deep breathing exercises and other mindfulness techniques are valuable tools for increasing awareness of one's emotional and physical states. Being mindful enables people to notice their feelings and bodily experiences without reacting immediately, promoting a more deliberate and calm reaction to stressors.

Journaling provides another avenue for self-reflection, allowing individuals to document patterns of anger, identify triggers, and explore the underlying emotions associated with specific situations. Through consistent journaling, individuals gain insight into their emotional landscape, uncovering recurring themes and contributing factors that can inform the development of effective anger management strategies.

Self-awareness, cultivated through mindfulness and reflective practices, is the cornerstone of breaking the cycle of reactive anger. By recognizing the interplay between physical and emotional triggers, individuals can intervene at earlier stages, preventing the escalation of anger. This awareness empowers individuals to make intentional choices in responding to triggers by implementing coping strategies and communication skills or seeking support when needed.

Effective anger management strategies involve not only recognizing triggers but also developing a repertoire of coping mechanisms that address both the physical and emotional dimensions of anger. Progressive muscle relaxation and guided meditation are two examples of mind-body practices that can help reduce the physiological reactions linked to anger. These methods ease stress, encourage relaxation, and provide a barrier to prevent rage from worsening.

Cognitive strategies focus on challenging and reframing distorted thoughts that contribute to anger. By adopting a more balanced and rational perspective, individuals can alter the mental patterns that fuel emotional reactions. This process involves questioning the accuracy of one's thoughts, considering alternative interpretations, and consciously choosing more adaptive ways of thinking.

Communication skills, including assertiveness and active listening, are indispensable tools in anger management. When people communicate assertively, they may respectfully and clearly express their needs, feelings, and boundaries, which lessens the possibility that they will become angry about unfulfilled expectations or unresolved issues. Conversely, attentive listening reduces the impact of emotional triggers by fostering empathy and understanding in interpersonal connections.

Techniques for ending the vicious cycle of rage involve individual actions and the more prominent family or social environment. Collaboratively, family members or close friends can establish a shared awareness of triggers and cooperate to establish an atmosphere that promotes emotional health. A dedication to personal development, mutual respect, and open communication all support the social system's general resilience in identifying and reducing anger causes.

In conclusion, recognizing physical and emotional triggers is foundational to effective anger management and overall emotional well-being. Through self-awareness, individuals can unravel the intricate web of triggers contributing to anger, fostering a greater understanding of their dynamic landscape. Individuals can break the cycle of reactive anger by implementing proactive coping mechanisms, challenging distorted thoughts, and cultivating practical communication skills. This intentional and ongoing process empowers individuals to navigate anger more skillfully and contributes to creating a healthier and more harmonious emotional environment within themselves and their relationships.

Stress Management Techniques

Stress has become an omnipresent companion for many individuals in modern life's fast-paced and demanding landscape. Juggling work responsibilities, personal commitments, and the constant influx of information can create tension and unease. Adopting efficient stress management techniques becomes essential when considering the negative impacts of ongoing stress on one's physical and mental health. This section delves into a wide range of stress management strategies, including mindfulness exercises, physical activity, relaxation techniques, and lifestyle modifications that all work together to support resilience and general well-being.

With roots in ancient contemplative practices, mindfulness has become a potent stress-reduction tool in the modern era. Cultivating a heightened awareness of the current moment without passing judgment is the goal of mindfulness. Techniques like mindfulness walking, deep breathing, and meditation allow people to ground themselves in the here and now, ending the worrying and rumination cycle frequently following stressful situations. Through the practice of non-judgmental awareness of thoughts and sensations, mindfulness helps people respond to challenges more calmly and clearly.

One prominent mindfulness technique is mindfulness meditation, where individuals dedicate time to focus their attention on the breath or a specific point of awareness. This intentional focus helps quiet the mind, reduces dress-induced physiological responses, and promotes inner peace. Mindfulness meditation has been shown to alleviate immediate stress and contribute to long-term improvements in emotional well-being, attention, and overall resilience in facing life's challenges.

The Mind-Body Connection

Physical activity, including regular exercise, is a potent stress management technique with multifaceted benefits. Engaging in physical activity releases endorphins, the body's natural mood lifters, contributing to improved mood and reduced stress levels. Exercise also helps regulate the physiological responses associated with stress, such as elevated heart rate and cortisol levels. Whether through aerobic activities like running or swimming, strength training, or more mindful practices like yoga, physical activity provides a holistic approach to stress management, promoting both physical and mental well-being.

For instance, yoga offers a comprehensive method of reducing stress by fusing physical postures with meditation and breath control. Yoga's deliberate breathing and soft poses help people unwind and create a mind-body connection that reduces stress. Yoga's meditative elements promote present-moment awareness, which helps people become less reactive to stress and develop a more centered and balanced perspective.

Relaxation techniques, ranging from progressive muscle relaxation to guided imagery, provide individuals with tools to counteract the physiological responses to stress. By tensing and releasing various muscle groups, progressive muscle relaxation encourages physical relaxation and a commensurate state of mental tranquility. By encouraging people to picture serene and quiet settings, guided imagery helps them relax and shift their focus from stressful situations. These methods are easily obtainable and can be used on one's own, under the supervision of audio recordings, or by experts in stress management.

Diaphragmatic breathing, often known as breath control, is a potent relaxing method that modifies the body's stress reaction. By concentrating on deep, steady breaths that involve the diaphragm, people can trigger the relaxation response in their bodies, which lessens the adverse effects of stress on the nervous system. Regular diaphragmatic breathing practice produces a heightened awareness of one's breath as a tool for stress management in various settings and instantly induces a feeling of serenity.

Long-term stress management heavily relies on lifestyle changes. Since insufficient or disturbed sleep can increase stress levels, developing healthy sleep patterns is essential to stress management. Making enough time for good sleep promotes mental and physical resilience, improving the body's capacity to handle stress in daily life. Keeping a healthy, well-balanced diet also helps with general wellbeing since it gives the body the resources it needs to perform at its best under pressure.

Time management and setting realistic expectations are crucial lifestyle adjustments in the context of stress management. Individuals often succumb to stress when faced with overwhelming workloads or unrealistic demands. Learning to prioritize tasks, delegate responsibilities, and establish boundaries allows individuals to navigate their duties more effectively, reducing the likelihood of chronic stress. Setting realistic expectations for oneself and acknowledging limitations fosters a more compassionate and adaptive approach to life's challenges.

Social support, an often underestimated stress management technique, promotes resilience. Connecting with friends, family, or support groups provides an avenue for sharing experiences, gaining perspective, and receiving emotional support. The hormone oxytocin, which promotes emotions of trust and bonding and lessens stress, is also released in response to social interactions. Building a support system and fostering healthy connections are essential elements of an all-encompassing stress management plan.

Cognitive-behavioral therapy aims to change the beliefs and mental processes that lead to stress. By recognizing and combating negative thought patterns, including all-or-nothing thinking or catastrophizing, people can change how they see the world and learn to respond more appropriately to stress. With cognitive restructuring, frequently used in therapeutic contexts, people can replace stressful and illogical ideas with more sensible and helpful ones.

Biofeedback, a technique that provides individuals with real-time information about physiological processes, empowers them to influence their body's responses to stress consciously. Individuals gain insight into their physiological reactions by monitoring parameters such as heart rate, muscle tension, or skin temperature. Often guided by professionals, biofeedback sessions help individuals develop greater control over their bodily responses, promoting relaxation and stress reduction.

In conclusion, stress management is a multifaceted endeavor combining techniques to address stress's physical, mental, and lifestyle dimensions. Mindfulness practices, physical activity, relaxation techniques, lifestyle adjustments, and social support collectively cultivate resilience and well-being. Integrating these techniques into daily life empowers individuals to navigate stress more effectively, fostering a balanced and adaptive approach to the challenges of modern living. As individuals embrace a holistic understanding of stress management, they embark on a journey towards greater self-awareness, emotional well-being, and a more resilient response to the complexities of life.

Mindfulness and Parenting

Parenting, a profound and multifaceted journey, is often characterized by many responsibilities, challenges, and joys. In the whirlwind of daily tasks, it is easy for parents to become entangled in the demands of the present moment, navigating a complex web of emotions and responsibilities. Mindfulness, rooted in ancient contemplative practice, has emerged as a transformative tool for parents seeking to navigate the intricate terrain of parenting with more significant presence, compassion, and emotional resilience. This section explores the profound intersection of mindfulness and parenting, delving into how mindfulness practices enhance the parent-child relationship, promote emotional well-being, and empower parents to cultivate a more intentional and connected approach to raising children.

A heightened awareness of the present moment combined with an accepting and nonjudgmental mindset is what mindfulness entails. When it comes to parenting, mindfulness encourages parents to pay intentional attention to their kids and the moments that unfold in their family life with an open mind. By releasing themselves from the clutches of automatic responses, parents can respond to the ever-changing problems of parenting with more significant consideration and empathy when present intentionally.

One of the fundamental contributions of mindfulness to parenting is its ability to deepen the parent-child relationship. Parents create an emotional safety and connection environment by being fully present and attuned to their children. Mindful parenting involves listening to children, acknowledging their emotions and reacting to them in a sympathetic and perceptive manner. The foundation for a good attachment and emotional well-being is laid by this atonement, which strengthens the parent-child link by fostering a sense of trust and security.

Parenting with mindfulness can be especially beneficial at complex or conflicting times. Aware parents wait to respond to a problematic situation or their child's misbehaviour rather than acting impulsively. They can watch their feelings during this time and decide based on their values and long-term parenting objectives. In this sense, mindfulness acts as a protective barrier against reactive parenting, enabling parents to handle times of discipline with composure and moderation.

Mindfulness techniques like body scan exercises or mindful breathing allow parents to control their emotions and handle stress. There will always be times when being a parent causes frustration, tiredness, and excessive demands. Parenting with mindfulness enables them to identify these feelings without becoming overwhelmed. Parents can handle the ups and downs of parenthood with more emotional resilience by practicing mindfulness or centering themselves in the here and now.

A crucial aspect of mindful parenting is the cultivation of self-compassion. Parenting, with its inevitable imperfections and challenges, can evoke guilt, self-doubt, or inadequacy. Mindfulness encourages parents to approach themselves with the same kindness and understanding they extend to their children. Embracing self-compassion allows parents to recognize that they are not immune to mistakes, and the journey of parenting is marked by growth, learning, and the continuous effort to do one's best.

Mindfulness extends beyond individual practices to encompass the family environment as a whole. Mindful families prioritize shared moments of presence and connection. Whether through conscious meals, family walks, or bed rituals, these intentional moments create a sense of unity and strengthen familial bonds. Mindful families also embrace the "slow parenting" concept, advocating for a balanced and present approach that values quality time over quantity.

The benefits of mindfulness in parenting extend to children as well. Mindful parents' model emotional regulation, effective communication, and empathy, providing children with invaluable tools for navigating emotions and relationships. The attuned and responsive parenting style associated with mindfulness contributes to developing secure attachment, a crucial foundation for healthy socio-emotional development in children.

Mindfulness practices also support children in developing their self-regulation skills. Children learn to anchor themselves in the present moment, manage stress, and cultivate emotional resilience through age-appropriate mindfulness activities, such as mindful breathing or guided imagery. These practices empower children to navigate the challenges of growing up with greater self-awareness and a toolbox of coping mechanisms.

Incorporating mindfulness into parenting does not necessitate elaborate practices or lengthy sessions. Simple but powerful moments of the present can help i corporate mindfulness into everyday life. Small acts of mindfulness, like stopping to enjoy all together, paying attention during a conversation, or taking a moment to breathe together, add to a more purposeful and cohesive family dynamic.

Mindfulness also contributes to a more adaptive and flexible parenting mindset. Parenting often involves navigating uncertainties, unexpected challenges, and evolving developmental stages. Mindfulness encourages parents to approach these moments with an open and non-judgmental mindset, embracing the ever-changing nature of parenting. The ability to respond to challenges flexibly and resilient is a hallmark of mindful parenting.

Integrating mindfulness into parenting aligns with contemporary research highlighting its positive effects on mental health and well-being. Studies have demonstrated that mindfulness practices elicit symptoms of stress, anxiety, and depression in parents, creating a more emotionally supportive environment for both parents and children. The benefits also extend to the physical realm, with mindfulness shown to improve sleep quality and overall physiological health.

Mindfulness programs have become valuable tools for promoting children's emotional well-being and positive behavior in educational settings. Mindfulness-based school interventions teach children essential skills for emotional regulation, attentional control, and conflict resolution. By incorporating mindfulness into parenting, families can complement and reinforce these skills, creating a harmonious and supportive environment for children's development.

In conclusion, integrating mindfulness into parenting represents a profound and transformative approach to raising children. Mindfulness practices enhance the parent-child relationship, promote emotional well-being, and empower parents to navigate the complexities of parenting with more significant presence and intentionality. By cultivating a mindful parenting mindset, parents can contribute to their well-being and the development of resilient, self-aware, and emotionally intelligent children. As families embrace the principles of mindfulness, they embark on a journey that enriches the fabric of their shared experiences, fostering connection, understanding, and a deep sense of well-being.

CHAPTER III

Communication Strategies

Effective Listening Skills

Effective listening is a skill that transcends mere hearing; it is the art of understanding, empathizing, and connecting with others on a profound level. In a world saturated with information and constant stimuli, the ability to listen with intentionality has become a rare and invaluable trait. This section explores the multifaceted dimensions of practical listening skills, delving into the importance of active listening, empathetic understanding, and the transformative impact of genuine connection in both personal and professional contexts.

Active listening is at the heart of effective listening, a dynamic process that goes beyond passively hearing words to actively engaging with the speaker's message. Active listening involves providing full attention, processing the information, and responding thoughtfully. This deliberate engagement requires the listener to set aside internal distractions, such as preconceived notions or personal biases, and focus on the speaker's words and non-verbal cues. Active listening is not merely waiting for one's turn to speak but involves a genuine curiosity and openness to understanding the speaker's perspective.

Empathetic understanding is a crucial component of effective listening, as it requires the listener to not only grasp the content of the message but also appreciate the emotional nuances conveyed by the speaker. Empathy involves putting oneself in the speaker's shoes, recognizing their feelings, and responding genuinely. The listener establishes a secure and encouraging environment for the speaker to express oneself honestly by exhibiting empathy. By creating trust and solidifying the interpersonal connection, this emotional resonance helps people interact with each other more.

Effective listening is essential for productive teamwork, successful dispute resolution, and leadership in the workplace. Effective listeners can better comprehend their team members' wants and requirements, which fosters cooperation and trust. Active listening guarantees that different points of view are considered and fosters an inclusive atmosphere in team environments. Effective leadership is listening intently to subordinates, clients, and coworkers. This helps businesses function more successfully as a whole.

In interpersonal relationships, effective listening serves as the cornerstone of healthy communication. It nurtures understanding, reduces misunderstandings, and fosters a sense of validation for each person's experiences and emotions. Couples who practice active and empathetic listening are better equipped to navigate challenges, resolve conflicts, and strengthen their emotional connection. Parent-child relationships benefit significantly from effective listening, as parents attuned to their children's needs and feelings create a supportive and nurturing environment for healthy development.

While providing unprecedented connectivity, the digital age has also introduced challenges to effective listening. The prevalence of virtual communication, characterized by text messages, emails, and social media interactions, often needs more richness of face-to-face communication. Misinterpretations and misunderstandings can quickly arise without non-verbal cues and vocal nuances. As individuals navigate this digital landscape, cultivating practical listening skills becomes even more critical for building meaningful connections and avoiding the pitfalls of miscommunication.

Listening in the digital era also involves managing the constant influx of information from various sources. The ability to discern relevant information, filter out distractions, and prioritize active engagement with meaningful content is essential. As individuals consume vast amounts of information daily, honing practical listening skills enables them to extract valuable insights, make informed decisions, and engage meaningfully in online and offline conversations.

The practice of mindfulness dramatically aids the development of helpful listening abilities. To listen mindfully, one must remove distractions from their thoughts, focus entirely on the speaker, and listen to what they have to say. By encouraging people to notice their ideas without passing judgment, mindfulness lowers the possibility that listeners will create opinions or assumptions while the speaker is still speaking. People can improve their listening ability with attention and empathy by adding mindfulness.

Cultural competence is pivotal in effective listening, especially in diverse and multicultural settings. Understanding the cultural context, norms, and communication styles of others enhances the listener's ability to interpret messages accurately and respond appropriately. Cultural competence involves a willingness to learn, adapt, and approach conversations with sensitivity to the cultural backgrounds of those involved. Individuals enrich their listening skills by embracing cultural diversity and promoting inclusive and respectful communication.

The educational context emphasizes the importance of effective listening for students and educators. Students with strong listening skills are better positioned to grasp complex concepts, engage actively in classroom discussions, and perform academically. Educators, in turn, play a crucial role in modeling effective listening behaviors, creating an inclusive learning environment, and fostering a collaborative atmosphere. In educational settings, effective listening is a reciprocal process that enhances the learning experience for all participants.

Overcoming barriers to effective listening requires consciously identifying and addressing common pitfalls. These barriers include selective listening, where individuals only focus on aspects of the message that align with their existing beliefs; judgmental listening, characterized by forming opinions or evaluations before fully understanding the speaker's perspective; and defensive listening, where individuals perceive criticism and respond with defensiveness rather than openness. By recognizing and mitigating these barriers, individuals can pave the way for more meaningful and constructive communication.

While contributing to global connectivity, technology has also introduced distractions that hinder effective listening. Constant notifications, multitasking, and the temptation to check devices during conversations can undermine listening quality. Digital mindfulness, which involves setting boundaries for device use and prioritizing face-to-face interactions, helps individuals reclaim their attention and cultivate effective listening habits in the digital age.

Effective listening is a skill that can be developed and refined through intentional practice and self-reflection. Active listening exercises, role-playing scenarios, and feedback from peers or mentors allow individuals to hone their listening skills. Additionally, seeking out diverse perspectives, engaging in conversations with people from different backgrounds, and exposing oneself to various communication styles contribute to improving practical listening abilities.

In conclusion, effective listening is a transformative skill that transcends communication; it is the bridge that connects individuals, fosters understanding, and cultivates meaningful relationships. Active listening, empathetic understanding, and cultural competence form the bedrock of practical listening skills, influencing personal, professional, and educational domains. As individuals navigate the complexities of communication in the digital age, the timeless art of effective listening remains a powerful tool for fostering connection, promoting collaboration, and enriching the fabric of human interaction.

Assertive Communication

Effective communication is the cornerstone of successful interpersonal interactions, and within this realm, assertive communication stands out as a powerful and balanced approach. Respecting the rights and perspectives of others while being open and honest in expressing one's thoughts, feelings, and needs is a critical component of assertiveness. The many facets of assertive communication are examined in this part, along with its guiding principles, advantages, and real-world applications in interpersonal relationships, the workplace, and self-improvement.

Achieving a harmonious balance between passive and aggressive communication styles is the fundamental goal of assertive communication. Reluctance to voice one's wants or thoughts is known as passive communication, and it frequently results in emotions of frustration or being ignored. Aggressive communication, on the other hand, is characterized by forceful expression, frequently at the price of the thoughts and feelings of others. Finding a midway ground, assertiveness enables people to express their ideas and emotions with confidence and clarity while honoring the boundaries and viewpoints of others.

Practicing assertive communication requires a foundation of self-awareness and a willingness to express oneself authentically. This self-awareness involves recognizing one's feelings, needs, and values, the basis for assertive expression. It also entails understanding personal boundaries and the ability to communicate assertively within those boundaries. Individuals who cultivate self-awareness are better equipped to navigate the complexities of communication with a clear sense of purpose and authenticity.

One of the critical principles of assertive communication is the use of "I" statements. These statements focus on expressing personal feelings, thoughts, and needs without attributing blame or making accusatory statements. For example, saying, "I feel frustrated when deadlines are not communicated clearly," is more assertive than saying, "You never provide clear deadlines." "I" statements foster open communication by avoiding defensiveness and encouraging a collaborative approach to problem-solving.

Another essential component of forceful communication is active listening. It entails listening intently, analysing what they say, and answering wisely. Respecting the speaker's viewpoint through active listening promotes a more fruitful and sympathetic discussion of ideas. Active listening is a tool that people use in conjunction with assertive communication to build relationships and foster understanding.

Assertive communication also involves the skill of making explicit and specific requests. Influential individuals articulate their requests directly and unambiguously instead of relying on vague or implied needs expressions. This clarity empowers others to understand and respond to the expressed needs, fostering a more transparent and efficient communication process. For instance, stating, "I would appreciate it if you could provide feedback on my project by the end of the week," is more assertive than a general request for feedback.

In personal relationships, assertive communication contributes significantly to establishing healthy boundaries and resolving conflicts. Individuals who practice assertiveness in their relationships can better communicate their needs, express feelings, and navigate disagreements constructively. Assertiveness fosters an environment of mutual respect and understanding, allowing individuals to maintain their individuality while fostering a sense of connection and intimacy.

In contrast, passive communication in personal relationships may lead to unmet needs and unexpressed feelings, resulting in simmering resentment and frustration. On the other hand, aggressive communication can escalate conflicts, damage relationships, and create an atmosphere of hostility. By promoting open and honest expression, assertive communication paves the way for healthier and more fulfilling connections.

In the workplace, assertive communication is a valuable skill contributing to effective collaboration, conflict resolution, and professional development. Strong individuals are more likely to express their ideas, contribute to discussions, and advocate for their needs within a team or organizational setting. This proactive approach enhances team dynamics and fosters a culture of open communication.

Leaders who employ assertive communication principles create a positive work environment, encouraging employees to voice their opinions and concerns. Strong leaders also provide clear expectations, offer constructive feedback, and address conflicts promptly and transparently. This leadership style promotes a sense of trust and accountability, contributing to the overall success and well-being of the organization.

In contrast, passive communication in the workplace may lead to missed opportunities for career advancement, unaddressed concerns, and a lack of visibility within the organization. Aggressive communication, on the other hand, may create a hostile work environment, hinder collaboration, and damage professional relationships. Conversely, assertive communication equips people to handle the intricacies of the workplace with professionalism and confidence.

Self-development and personal growth benefit significantly from assertive communication. Individuals who practice assertiveness are more likely to set and pursue personal goals, express their needs in various aspects of life, and advocate for their well-being. Assertiveness fosters a sense of agency and empowerment, enabling individuals to navigate life's challenges with resilience and a positive mindset.

In contrast, passive individuals may struggle to assert their needs, leading to unfulfilled aspirations and a sense of powerlessness. Aggressive individuals may experience strained relationships and resistance from others, hindering their personal and professional growth. By fostering self-advocacy and empowerment, assertive communication allows individuals to navigate the journey of self-discovery and self-improvement more effectively.

Overcoming barriers to assertive communication involves addressing common obstacles such as fear of conflict, low self-esteem, or the desire to please others at the expense of one's needs. Building assertiveness skills may involve seeking support from counsellors, attending assertiveness training workshops, or practicing assertive behaviors in low-stakes situations. People can fully realize the benefits of effective communication in various contexts by identifying and removing these obstacles.

In conclusion, assertive communication is a transformative and empowering approach that enhances interpersonal relationships, professional interactions, and personal growth. The principles of assertiveness, including using "I" statements, active listening, and explicit requests, contribute to open and respectful communication. In personal relationships, assertiveness fosters intimacy and understanding. In the workplace, it enhances collaboration and leadership effectiveness. For personal development, assertive communication is vital for self-advocacy and empowerment. As individuals embrace assertiveness, they unlock the potential for more confident, respectful, and fulfilling connections in every facet of life.

Teaching Children Emotional Expression

During the formative years of childhood, children acquire fundamental skills that establish the groundwork for their social and emotional development. Central to this development is the ability to express and navigate emotions effectively. Teaching children emotional expression is crucial to fostering emotional intelligence, empathy, and resilience. This section explores the importance of guiding children in understanding and expressing their emotions, examining strategies, benefits, and the long-term impact of emotional expression on children's overall development.

Children experience a wide range of emotions from a very young age. However, they may not possess the vocabulary or understanding to articulate these feelings. Teaching emotional expression involves providing children with the tools to identify, label, and communicate emotions. This process introduces basic emotions such as happiness, sadness, anger, fear, and surprise. Through conversations, stories, or visual aids, children can start associating words with their emotional experiences, enabling them to express themselves more effectively.

Storytelling emerges as a powerful tool in teaching children about emotions. Narratives allow children to relate to fictional characters who experience various feelings, providing a platform for discussing emotions and their impact. By connecting emotions to relatable stories, children learn that they are expected to experience a range of feelings and that these feelings can be expressed and understood. This narrative approach fosters empathy, encouraging children to recognize and respect the emotions of others.

In a child's development, modelling emotional expression is equally important. Youngsters pick up a lot of knowledge from seeing peers and adults behave. When parents exhibit healthy emotional expression, such as noticing and expressing their emotions, children are likelier to follow suit. Establishing an atmosphere where people freely talk about their feelings and provide positive role models for handling them lays the groundwork for children to grow in their capacity for emotional expression.

Children can creatively express their feelings through artistic endeavours. When verbal speech becomes difficult, youngsters might externalize their emotions through creative expression through drawing, painting, or other mediums. Additionally, art offers a material manifestation of feelings, allowing grown-ups to discuss their artwork with kids. Through this process, emotional expression is improved, and the idea that all emotions are real and have a variety of expressions is reaffirmed.

Encouraging open communication about emotions is crucial in creating a supportive environment. Children need to feel that expressing their feelings is accepted and encouraged. Establishing a routine of checking in with children about their emotions and actively listening to their responses cultivates a sense of trust and safety. This practice normalizes sharing emotions, fostering a culture where children feel heard and understood.

Teaching children about emotional regulation goes hand in hand with emotional expression. Emotional regulation involves recognizing and managing one's emotions in a socially acceptable way that does not harm oneself or others. Through guidance and modeling, children can learn various strategies for emotional regulation, such as deep breathing, counting to ten, or taking a break. These techniques empower children to navigate challenging emotions independently, promoting self-awareness and resilience.

Empathy, a cornerstone of healthy social interactions, is closely linked to emotional expression. When children can identify and understand their own emotions, they are better equipped to recognize and empathize with the feelings of others. Activities that encourage perspective-taking, such as discussing situations from different points of view or engaging in role-playing, enhance children's ability to connect with the emotions of their peers. Empathy fosters positive relationships and contributes to the development of strong social bonds.

The benefits of teaching emotional expression extend beyond immediate social interactions; they profoundly impact children's mental health and overall well-being. Research suggests that children who are adept at expressing and regulating their emotions are less prone to behavioral issues, anxiety, and depression. These children exhibit higher levels of self-esteem, engage more effectively in social relationships, and demonstrate more tremendous academic success. By equipping children with emotional expression skills, we provide them with a valuable foundation for navigating life's challenges.

Furthermore, emotional expression is necessary for developing emotional intelligence, which is essential for success in various spheres of life. The abilities to identify and comprehend one's feelings, sympathize with others, and successfully negotiate social complexity are all included in emotional intelligence. Youngsters with vital emotional intelligence are more capable of managing stress, using aggressive language, and building healthy relationships. Early emotional expression instruction helps children develop emotional intelligence and equips them with a valuable skill set for success as adults in their personal and professional lives.

However, the process of teaching emotional expression is challenging. Cultural and societal influences, gender stereotypes, and individual differences in temperament can impact how children perceive and express emotions. Creating an inclusive and culturally sensitive approach that recognizes and respects diverse emotional expression styles is crucial. Furthermore, eliminating the stigmas attached to particular emotions, like vulnerability or melancholy, guarantees that kids feel free to express emotions.

In summary, a child's overall growth depends on their ability to articulate their emotions. We help children develop emotional intelligence, empathy, and resilience by giving them the skills to recognize, comprehend, and communicate their feelings. Children feel empowered to express themselves genuinely in a supportive environment created through storytelling, modeling, artistic activities, and open communication. The advantages transcend childhood, impacting mental well-being, interpersonal relationships, and achievement in diverse spheres of life. By spending money on training kids to communicate their emotions, we give them a lifetime skill that improves their emotional health and increases their ability to form meaningful relationships.

CHAPTER IV

Setting Realistic Expectations

Managing Parental Expectations

Parenthood is a transformative and profound journey that brings joy, challenges, and many emotions. Amidst the anticipation and excitement, parents often form expectations that influence their perceptions of the parenting experience. Managing parental expectations is crucial to fostering a healthy and resilient approach to parenthood. This section explores the dynamics of parental expectations, the impact on the parent-child relationship, and strategies for navigating parenthood's complexities with realism and adaptability.

Parental expectations often arise from a combination of societal norms, cultural influences, personal values, and past experiences. The desire to be a "perfect" parent, meet certain milestones, or replicate one's own positive experiences can contribute to forming expectations. While aspirations for a positive and nurturing parenting experience are natural, unrealistic or rigid expectations may lead to disappointment, stress, and inadequacy when reality deviates from these ideals.

One familiar expectation parent may grapple with is the idea of a perfect, harmonious family life. The portrayal of idealized family dynamics in media and societal narratives can create an unrealistic benchmark for parents. The reality of parenthood often involves moments of chaos, unpredictability, and imperfection. Managing the expectations of an idyllic family life requires embracing the messiness of parenting, acknowledging the ups and downs, and cultivating resilience in the face of challenges.

Another prevalent expectation centres around a parent's role in shaping their child's future. Parents may carry the weight of expectations about their child's achievements, behaviour, or career choices. While it is natural for parents to aspire to provide the best opportunities for their children, unrealistic expectations can lead to excessive pressure and strained parent-child relationships. Recognizing and adjusting these expectations involves acknowledging the individuality of each child, embracing their unique strengths and challenges, and fostering an environment that encourages growth rather than perfection.

The notion of a seamless work-life balance is an expectation that often challenges parents, particularly in the modern era. Balancing career responsibilities with the demands of parenting can be complex, and the expectation of effortlessly juggling both realms can contribute to feelings of guilt or inadequacy. Managing this expectation requires acknowledging the need for flexibility, seeking support when necessary, and prioritizing self-care to maintain a sustainable balance.

Setting Realistic Expectations

The developmental milestones of children are also subject to parental expectations. Unrealistic expectations about when a kid should reach particular milestones, like walking, talking, or intellectual ability, might be fuelled by comparisons with other children or societal norms. Recognizing and respecting the unique pace of each child's development, along with seeking guidance from healthcare professionals, enables parents to embrace a more realistic and supportive approach.

The impact of parental expectations on the parent-child relationship is profound. Unrealistic or rigid expectations can create a sense of pressure and performance anxiety for both parents and children. Children may internalize the expectations imposed upon them, leading to feelings of inadequacy or rebellion. Moreover, the strain caused by unmet expectations can erode the foundation of trust and communication within the parent-child relationship.

Conversely, parents who manage expectations flexibly and with realism cultivate a more open and supportive relationship with their children. Creating an environment where children feel accepted for who they are, rather than for meeting predefined expectations, fosters a sense of security and self-esteem. Mutual understanding, empathy, and readiness to modify expectations in light of parents' and kids' changing needs and abilities are essential to solid parent-child interactions.

Strategies for managing parental expectations involve a combination of self-awareness, communication, and adaptability. First and foremost, parents benefit from reflecting on their expectations and questioning their origins. By understanding the source of expectations, parents can differentiate between realistic aspirations and those influenced by external pressures or unrealistic ideals. Self-awareness provides a foundation for intentional and mindful parenting.

Open communication within the family is paramount for managing expectations effectively. Establishing a dialogue where parents and children can express their thoughts, feelings, and concerns fosters a sense of transparency and mutual understanding. Children benefit from knowing that their parents have realistic expectations and are willing to support them through challenges. Honest communication also allows parents to adapt their expectations based on their children's evolving needs and capacities.

Cultivating resilience is a vital component of managing parental expectations. Resilient parents recognize that parenthood involves uncertainties, setbacks, and continuous learning. Embracing a mindset that values the journey over perfection enables parents to navigate challenges with adaptability and patience. Resilience involves seeking support when needed, acknowledging mistakes, and learning from experiences to foster personal growth and a healthier parent-child relationship.

Mindfulness practices contribute significantly to managing parental expectations. Mindfulness involves being present in the moment without judgment, allowing parents to respond to situations with greater clarity and intentionality. Parents who practice mindful parenting are encouraged to let go of their need for perfection, find delight in the little things in life, and address problems with composure. Mindfulness provides a valuable tool for breaking free from the cycle of unrealistic expectations and fostering a more grounded and fulfilling parenting experience.

Seeking support from a community of parents or professionals can be instrumental in managing parental expectations. Sharing experiences, insights, and challenges with others with similar concerns provides a sense of validation and reduces feelings of isolation. Parenting is a collective journey; exchanging support and advice contributes to a more informed and resilient parenting approach.

Parental expectations can make parenting more satisfying and peaceful if handled realistically and flexibly. Embracing the imperfections of parenthood, fostering open communication, cultivating resilience, practicing mindfulness, and seeking support all contribute to a healthier approach to parental expectations. Ultimately, the goal is not to eliminate expectations but to reshape them into a framework that allows flexibility, growth, and a deeper connection with one's children. With its joys and challenges, Parenthood becomes a journey marked by acceptance, understanding, and the resilience to adapt to the ever-changing landscape of family life.

Age-Appropriate Behavior

Understanding age-appropriate behavior is essential for parents, educators, and caregivers as they navigate the intricate landscape of child development. Children progress through various stages of growth, each marked by distinct physical, cognitive, and emotional milestones. Recognizing and respecting age-appropriate behavior involves acknowledging the diversity of individual variations within each age group and creating an environment that nurtures healthy development. This section explores the significance of age-appropriate behavior, the influence of developmental stages, and the importance of considering individual differences in fostering positive child outcomes.

Age-appropriate behavior is closely linked to developmental stages, encompassing the physical, social, emotional, and cognitive changes children undergo as they grow. Infants, for example, exhibit age-appropriate behavior when they respond to stimuli, establish basic motor skills, and form early attachments with caregivers. Toddlers explore their surroundings, develop language skills, and assert their independence. Preschoolers engage in imaginative play, refine motor skills, and develop social skills through peer interactions. School-age children further expand their social networks, refine cognitive abilities, and create a sense of identity. Adolescents undergo significant emotional and mental changes as they transition into adulthood. Understanding these developmental stages provides a framework for assessing and appreciating age-appropriate behavior.

The influence of developmental milestones on behavior is evident in the diverse ways children express themselves at different ages. For instance, a toddler's tantrums may be a developmentally appropriate response to frustration, as they are still learning to regulate their emotions. Conversely, a school-age child's desire for autonomy and mastery of specific skills aligns with their developmental stage.

Setting Realistic Expectations

Adolescents' exploration of identity, values, and independence reflects the natural progression toward adulthood. Recognizing these age-related behaviors allows adults to respond with empathy and understanding, creating a supportive environment that nurtures optimal development.

It is crucial to note that while developmental milestones provide a general framework, individual variations play a significant role in shaping behavior. Children within the same age group may exhibit differences in temperament, learning styles, and socio-cultural influences that impact their behavior. Some children may reach particular milestones earlier or later than their peers, and these variations contribute to the rich tapestry of human development. A child's unique combination of genetic factors, environmental influences, and personal experiences contributes to the individuality of their behavior. Therefore, embracing and accommodating these differences is critical to promoting each child's well-being and fostering a positive sense of self.

The role of caregivers, parents, and educators in guiding age-appropriate behavior is pivotal. Creating an environment that supports healthy development involves providing age-appropriate stimuli, opportunities for exploration, and positive reinforcement. Caregivers can facilitate age-appropriate behavior by offering age-specific toys, activities, and challenges that align with a child's current developmental stage. Moreover, a secure and nurturing atmosphere fosters trust, emotional regulation, and healthy attachment, which are essential to age-appropriate behavior.

Discipline and guidance strategies should also be tailored to the child's developmental stage. Effective discipline involves setting clear and consistent expectations, providing developmentally appropriate consequences, and offering positive reinforcement for desired behaviors. For instance, a preschooler may respond well to a time-out due to not sharing, while a teenager might benefit more from discussing responsibility and accountability. Understanding the child's developmental level ensures that discipline is constructive and respectful of their evolving capacities.

Promoting age-appropriate behavior extends beyond the home to educational settings. Teachers play a crucial role in creating classrooms catering to students' diverse needs at various developmental stages. Lesson plans, activities, and expectations should align with the cognitive and social capabilities of the students. Providing age-appropriate challenges and opportunities for exploration allows students to engage with the learning process effectively. Additionally, educators should be attuned to individual differences within the classroom, recognizing that each child brings unique strengths and challenges.

In fostering age-appropriate behavior, the importance of positive role modelling cannot be overstated. Adults influence a child's behavior, and their actions, attitudes, and responses shape the child's understanding of appropriate conduct. Fostering a pleasant behavioural environment is facilitated by demonstrating empathy, effective communication, and problem-solving techniques. Caregivers and educators must model the values and behaviors they want to establish in the younger generation since children often imitate the conduct they see in adults.

Working together, parents, educators, and mental health specialists can effectively address behavioral difficulties. Some behavioral issues could be signs of emotional difficulties, learning challenges, or developmental problems. Getting expert advice enables a thorough evaluation of a child's needs and the creation of focused interventions that promote appropriate behavior for their age. Early intervention and collaboration among many stakeholders influence positive results for children with behavioral issues.

While age-appropriate behavior provides a helpful framework, it is crucial to recognize the importance of individual differences and the potential impact of external factors on behavior. Children with diverse abilities, backgrounds, and experiences may exhibit variations in their developmental trajectories. Factors such as family dynamics, socioeconomic conditions, and cultural influences contribute to the complexity of each child's behavioral profile. Therefore, embracing a holistic and inclusive perspective ensures that interventions and support systems address the unique needs of every child.

In conclusion, understanding and fostering age-appropriate behavior involves recognizing the influence of developmental stages, acknowledging individual variations, and creating an environment that supports healthy growth. Caregivers, parents, and educators are pivotal in guiding children through their developmental journey, offering age-specific challenges, positive reinforcement, and effective discipline. By promoting a positive behavioral environment that considers developmental milestones and individual differences, adults contribute to the holistic well-being of children, nurturing their potential and shaping their positive engagement with the world.

Embracing Imperfection

In a society that often glorifies perfection, embracing imperfection is a counterbalance—a profound philosophy that encourages individuals to find beauty and strength in their flaws, mistakes, and vulnerabilities. The quest for perfection can be a draining and unreachable objective that breeds worry, insecurity, and a persistent dread of failing. In contrast, embracing imperfection invites a shift in perspective that acknowledges the inherent humanness of making mistakes, experiencing setbacks, and not always meeting societal or personal expectations. This section explores the significance of embracing imperfection as a transformative and empowering approach to life, emphasizing its impact on authenticity, resilience, and personal growth.

At the heart of embracing imperfection lies the recognition that perfection is an illusion. The societal pressure to conform to flawless standards, whether in appearance, achievements, or relationships, can create an insidious cycle of comparison and self-judgment. The quest for perfection often leads to a distorted self-image, where individuals must present an idealized version of themselves, hiding behind a facade of flawlessness. Accepting flaws breaks down this façade and enables people to connect with their true selves and develop a true sense of self.

Setting Realistic Expectations

Authenticity, a cornerstone of embracing imperfection, involves embracing one's true self, complete with strengths and weaknesses. It entails acknowledging and expressing genuine emotions, thoughts, and experiences without fear of judgment. Authentic individuals foster deeper connections with others, as their openness and vulnerability create an atmosphere of trust and relatability. By embracing imperfection, individuals liberate themselves from the constraints of societal expectations and embrace the beauty of their authentic selves.

The process of becoming resilient is entwined with learning to accept imperfections. The ability to overcome obstacles, disappointments, or setbacks with renewed strength and insight is known as resilience. Embracing imperfection reframes failures as opportunities for learning and growth rather than as indicators of inadequacy. When individuals let go of the fear of making mistakes, they become more resilient in the face of adversity. This resilience allows them to navigate life's uncertainties with adaptability and perseverance.

In the realm of personal relationships, embracing imperfection fosters healthier and more authentic connections. In romantic relationships, the pressure to be a flawless partner can create unrealistic expectations and hinder genuine intimacy. Embracing imperfection allows individuals to share their vulnerabilities and openly communicate their needs and fears. This vulnerability strengthens the bond between partners as they navigate the complexities of a relationship with empathy, understanding, and mutual support.

Parenting, too, is profoundly influenced by the philosophy of embracing imperfection. Parents who recognize and accept their imperfections create a more nurturing and forgiving environment for their children. This approach instills in children a healthier perspective on failure and imperfection, equipping them with essential life skills and promoting a positive self-image.

The workplace is another arena where the pressure for perfection can be pervasive. Employees striving for perfection may experience burnout, anxiety, and diminished creativity. Embracing imperfection in the workplace involves recognizing that innovation often emerges from trial and error. Creating a culture that values mistakes as learning opportunities fosters a more collaborative and adaptive work environment. It allows individuals to take risks, share creative ideas, and approach challenges with a growth mindset.

The media's portrayal of perfection, amplified by social media, contributes to the pervasive pressure individuals feel to conform to idealized standards. Embracing imperfection challenges the unrealistic narratives the media perpetuates, encouraging individuals to celebrate their unique qualities rather than striving for an unattainable ideal. When used consciously, social media platforms can become spaces for authentic self-expression, genuine connection, and the celebration of diverse perspectives.

The path to embracing imperfection involves cultivating self-compassion—a compassionate and understanding attitude toward oneself in the face of failure or adversity. Self-compassion allows individuals to acknowledge their imperfections without harsh self-judgment. It involves treating oneself with the same kindness and understanding that one would offer to a friend facing similar challenges. Through self-compassion, individuals develop a more resilient and positive relationship with themselves, creating a foundation for embracing imperfection.

Engaging in mindfulness activities is also essential to the process of accepting imperfections. Mindfulness involves being present in the moment and non-judgmentally observing thoughts and feelings. By practicing mindfulness, individuals can cultivate awareness of their internal dialogue and challenge perfectionistic tendencies. Mindfulness encourages a more accepting and compassionate relationship with oneself, fostering an appreciation for the richness of life's imperfections.

A pivotal aspect of embracing imperfection is reframing failures as stepping stones to growth. Failures and mistakes are inherent parts of the human experience, offering valuable lessons and opportunities for self-discovery. This mindset shift transforms setbacks into catalysts for personal and professional development.

Embracing imperfection is not synonymous with complacency or a lack of ambition. Instead, it involves setting realistic goals, acknowledging limitations, and recognizing that the journey toward self-improvement is ongoing. Striving for excellence and pursuing goals becomes a positive and motivated endeavour rather than a source of unrelenting pressure. This approach allows individuals to appreciate their progress and celebrate achievements without being overshadowed by perceived shortcomings.

Society, too, plays a role in fostering an environment that supports the philosophy of embracing imperfection. The dismantling of societal expectations and norms that perpetuate the pursuit of perfection requires collective efforts. By challenging unrealistic beauty standards, academic pressures, and rigid gender roles, society can create space for diverse expressions of identity and success. Celebrating authenticity and imperfection at a societal level contributes to the well-being of individuals and promotes a more inclusive and compassionate culture.

In conclusion, embracing imperfection is a transformative philosophy that challenges the relentless pursuit of perfection in various aspects of life. Individuals cultivate authenticity, resilience, and a positive sense of self by acknowledging and celebrating one's flaws, mistakes, and vulnerabilities. This mindset shift extends to personal relationships, parenting, the workplace, and societal expectations, fostering healthier dynamics and a more compassionate culture. Accepting imperfection doesn't mean settling for mediocrity; instead, it means appreciating the intrinsic beauty of the flawed path that defines being human—a path filled with development, education, and diverse experiences that mold us into the people we indeed are.

CHAPTER V

Anger-Management Techniques for Parents

Deep Breathing and Relaxation Exercises

In the fast-paced rhythm of modern life, marked by constant demands and pressures, the significance of cultivating moments of calm and relaxation cannot be overstated. Deep breathing and relaxation exercises emerge as invaluable tools in this pursuit, offering a gateway to a harmonious connection between the mind and body. Rooted in ancient practices from various cultures and embraced by contemporary wellness approaches, these techniques provide individuals with accessible and effective means to manage stress, enhance mental well-being, and promote overall health. This section explores the profound impact of deep breathing and relaxation exercises, unravelling how these practices contribute to stress reduction, emotional balance, and a heightened sense of self-awareness.

At the core of deep breathing and relaxation exercises lies an understanding of the intricate relationship between the mind and the body. The physiological and psychological responses to stress, commonly known as the fight-or-flight response, trigger a cascade of reactions, including increased heart rate, shallow breathing, and heightened muscle tension. Deep breathing counterbalances this stress response, activating the parasympathetic nervous system—often called the "rest and digest" system. By intentionally slowing down their breathing and engaging in relaxation exercises, individuals elicit a relaxation response that counteracts the physiological effects of stress, fostering a state of calmness and balance.

One of the fundamental elements of deep breathing exercises is diaphragmatic breathing, also known as belly or abdominal respiration. Using this method, take a deep breath through your nostrils. you are allowing the diaphragm to expand, and exhaling slowly through pursed lips. Better oxygen and carbon dioxide exchange is encouraged by diaphragmatic breathing, which also enhances the diaphragm's use—a big muscle located between the chest and abdomen. This deliberate, conscious breathing improves oxygen flow and promotes feelings of contentment and calm.

Mindful breathing, a central component of relaxation exercises, draws inspiration from mindfulness and meditation practices. It involves bringing full attention to the present moment, focusing on the inhalation and exhalation of each breath. Mindful breathing encourages individuals to observe their thoughts without judgment and gently bring their attention back to the breath when distractions arise. This heightened awareness cultivates a sense of mindfulness, promoting mental clarity, stress reduction, and an increased capacity to manage challenging situations.

Progressive muscle relaxation (PMR) is another effective relaxation technique that complements deep breathing exercises. Developed by Dr. Edmund Jacobson in the early 20th century, PMR involves systematically tensing and relaxing different muscle groups throughout the body. People can release muscle tension and achieve profound physical and mental serenity through this method. It also helps people become more attuned to the bodily sensations of tension and relaxation.

Deep breathing and relaxation techniques may help people de-stress instantly, but they have also been linked to many other positive effects on the body and mind. Research suggests that regular engagement in these techniques can contribute to lowered blood pressure, improved immune function, and enhanced cardiovascular health. Moreover, the psychological benefits include reduced anxiety, improved mood, and better sleep quality. The mind-body connection fostered by deep breathing and relaxation exercises provides a holistic approach to well-being, acknowledging the intricate interplay between mental and physical health.

Acute or chronic stress is a pervasive element of contemporary life, affecting individuals from various walks of life. The workplace, in particular, has become a common source of stress for many, with demanding schedules, high expectations, and the constant connectivity facilitated by technology. Deep breathing and relaxation exercises offer a practical and accessible solution for managing workplace stress. Integrating short breaks for deep breathing or incorporating mindfulness into daily routines empowers individuals to navigate work-related challenges with greater resilience and composure.

Educational settings also stand to benefit from the integration of deep breathing and relaxation exercises. Students facing academic pressures and the demands of a rapidly changing educational landscape often experience heightened stress levels. Incorporating these practices into the school environment can create a supportive atmosphere that fosters emotional regulation, concentration, and overall well-being. Mindful breathing exercises have been introduced in schools as part of mindfulness-based programs, contributing to improved focus, emotional balance, and a positive classroom culture.

The relationship between deep breathing and relaxation exercises and mental health is particularly noteworthy. Anxiety and depression, prevalent mental health challenges, can be significantly impacted by the regular practice of these techniques. Deep breathing and relaxation exercises offer individuals a tangible and empowering tool to manage symptoms, reduce the physiological effects of stress, and cultivate a more positive mental outlook. Moreover, these practices align with therapeutic approaches such as mindfulness-based cognitive therapy (MBCT), which integrates mindfulness practices with cognitive-behavioral therapy to prevent the recurrence of depressive episodes.

Chronic pain conditions, often intertwined with stress and tension, also see relief by incorporating relaxation exercises. Conditions like fibromyalgia, migraines, and tension headaches have been shown to respond positively to relaxation techniques. By reducing muscle tension, promoting a sense of calm, and altering the perception of pain, deep breathing exercises become valuable adjuncts to the comprehensive management of chronic pain.

Pregnancy and childbirth represent periods in a woman's life where the benefits of relaxation exercises are particularly pronounced. Prenatal yoga, deep breathing, and progressive muscle relaxation are commonly recommended to expectant mothers as ways to manage stress, alleviate discomfort, and prepare for childbirth. Additionally, relaxation techniques promote a positive birth experience by promoting a calm and focused mindset, facilitating pain management, and fostering a supportive birthing environment.

Incorporating deep breathing and relaxation exercises into daily routines does not require extensive time commitments or specialized equipment. Simple practices, such as taking short breaks for mindful breathing, incorporating diaphragmatic breathing into moments of stress, or dedicating a few minutes to progressive muscle relaxation, can yield substantial benefits. These approaches are appropriate for people of various ages, fitness levels, and lifestyles because they are easily accessible.

Technological advancements have also facilitated the integration of deep breathing and relaxation exercises into digital platforms. Mobile applications, online resources, and virtual classes offer guided sessions, breathing exercises, and relaxation techniques tailored to individual preferences. These digital tools provide flexibility and convenience, allowing individuals to incorporate relaxation practices regardless of location or daily schedule.

While deep breathing and relaxation exercises offer profound benefits, it is crucial to acknowledge that individual preferences and responses vary. What works for one person may not resonate with another. Therefore, exploring different techniques, seeking guidance from qualified instructors, and adapting practices to individual needs enhance the effectiveness of these exercises. The emphasis is not on perfection or adherence to a rigid routine but on cultivating a personalized and sustainable approach to relaxation.

In conclusion, deep breathing and relaxation exercises are potent allies in the quest for well-being in the face of life's stresses and challenges. By harnessing the mind-body connection, these practices provide a gateway to stress reduction, emotional balance, and increased self-awareness. For those looking to improve their general health and vitality, deep breathing and relaxation techniques are helpful and easily accessible tools. These include managing chronic pain, managing workplace stress, addressing mental health issues, and easing the transitions of pregnancy. Slowing down, paying attention to our breath, and savouring peaceful moments become both a luxury and an essential component of a well-rounded and prosperous life as we traverse the complexity of modern living.

Time-Outs for Parents

Undoubtedly, one of the most fulfilling and challenging jobs a person can have is becoming a parent. From the sleepless nights of infancy to the tumultuous teenage years, parents navigate many emotions, responsibility, and constant adjustments. In this intricate dance of nurturing and guiding, it becomes imperative for parents to recognize the importance of self-care. Amidst the demands of daily life, the concept of "time-outs for parents" emerges as a valuable strategy, offering moments of respite, reflection, and rejuvenation. This section explores the significance of time-outs for parents, delving into the potential benefits, practical implementation, and the profound impact these pauses can have on the well-being of both parents and their families.

Parenting is a multifaceted journey that demands continuous emotional, physical, and mental engagement. The unrelenting nature of parenting responsibilities, coupled with the evolving needs of children, can lead to exhaustion, feeling overwhelmed, and burnout. Recognizing the signs of parental stress is the first step in understanding the necessity of time-outs. Symptoms such as irritability, persistent fatigue, changes in sleep patterns, and a decline in emotional well-being signal the importance of prioritizing self-care. Time-outs for parents serve as a preventive and restorative measure, allowing individuals to step back, recharge, and return to their parental roles with increased resilience and clarity.

The term "time-out" is often associated with its application in child discipline, where a child is temporarily removed from a challenging situation to regain composure. When applied to parents, the concept shifts from discipline to self-care, offering an opportunity to temporarily step away from the demands of parenting. These breaks do not indicate neglect or avoidance but are a proactive approach to maintaining parental well-being and mental health. By acknowledging the need for moments of solitude and rejuvenation, parents can foster a healthier and more sustainable approach to their roles.

Time-outs for parents include various forms of self-care, ranging from brief moments of solitude to more extended breaks. Taking quick pauses can be going outdoors to get some fresh air, practicing deep breathing for a little while, or doing a short mindfulness activity. Extended vacations could include planning a day off to explore particular hobbies, planning a weekend getaway, or engaging in enjoyable and stimulating activities. The secret is to customize time-outs based on personal tastes and requirements, understanding that self-care is an individual's journey.

The benefits of time-outs for parents extend beyond individual well-being; they create a positive and nurturing family environment. When parents prioritize self-care, they model the importance of maintaining mental and emotional balance. Children observe their parents as individuals with needs, boundaries, and coping mechanisms, fostering a healthy understanding of self-care from an early age. Moreover, parents who practice self-care are better equipped to handle parenting challenges, respond to children with patience and empathy, and maintain a more harmonious family dynamic.

Implementing time-outs for parents requires a shift in mindset—an acknowledgment that self-care is not a luxury but a fundamental aspect of effective parenting. Overcoming guilt or feelings of selfishness is crucial; parents must recognize that caring for oneself enhances the capacity to care for others. Communication within a parenting partnership is vital to ensure that both partners understand and support each other's need for time-outs. Collaboratively establishing a routine that accommodates breaks for each parent can contribute to a more balanced and supportive parenting dynamic.

Incorporating time-outs into daily routines involves planning and commitment. Creating a schedule that includes moments for self-care, designating specific days for more extended breaks, and communicating these plans with co-parents or support networks are essential. Building a support network for single parents through friends, family, or community resources, becomes paramount. It takes a village to raise a child, and acknowledging one's need for support and respite is a strength, not a weakness.

Practical strategies for time-outs can vary based on individual preferences and circumstances. For some, incorporating mindfulness practices into daily routines, such as meditation or yoga, can be a brief yet impactful break. Others may find solace in hobbies, reading, or nature. Finding things to do that make you happy, relaxed, and fulfilled is the key. Effective time-outs can also be facilitated by designating a physical area in the house for quiet thought, such as a private sanctuary or a pleasant corner.

The workplace, frequently a significant cause of stress for parents, is essential to the success of time-out policies. Parents can more effectively incorporate self-care into their daily routines when they have flexible work schedules, telecommuting possibilities, and family-friendly policies. Organizations that promote a culture of understanding and support for parental obligations enhance employees' general wellbeing.

Given the frequency of parental stress and burnout, the effects of time-outs on parents' mental health are significant. Long-term stress can worsen mental health conditions like anxiety and depression, which can both have an impact on people's general wellbeing and the quality of parent-child relationships. Time-outs allow parents to process feelings, obtain perspective, and create coping mechanisms while acting as a buffer against the cumulative effects of stress. Regular self-care routines are linked to elevated resilience, happier moods, and more optimistic parenting perspectives.

While the benefits of time-outs or parents are substantial, it is essential to recognize potential barriers to implementation. Common obstacles include guilt, perceived societal expectations, and the belief that effective parenting requires constant sacrifice. Overcoming these barriers involves challenging societal narratives around parenthood, prioritizing personal well-being without guilt, and reframing self-care as an integral aspect of effective parenting. Education and advocacy around the importance of parental self-care contribute to a cultural shit that normalizes and supports these practices.

In conclusion, time-outs for parents emerge as a vital component of the parenting journey—an intentional and proactive approach to maintaining individual well-being and fostering a positive family environment. Parents can better negotiate parenting challenges with grace and resilience by identifying stress symptoms, prioritizing self-care, and scheduling moments of respite into daily routines. The transformative impact of time-outs extends beyond the individual, influencing the family dynamic and creating a nurturing and balanced home environment. In embracing the concept of time-outs, parents embark on a journey of self-discovery, self-compassion, and the cultivation of a more sustainable and fulfilling approach to the profound responsibility of raising the next generation.

Journaling and Reflective Practices

In the intricate tapestry of human experience, the art of introspection holds a profound significance. Journaling becomes an effective tool for people who want to delve deeply into their ideas, feelings, and experiences as a reflective practice. Rooted in ancient traditions and embraced by contemporary psychology, journaling provides a structured space for self-expression, self-discovery, and personal growth. This section delves into the multifaceted realm of journaling and reflective practices, unravelling the psychological benefits, practical approaches, and transformative impact these intentional exercises can have on individuals' well-being and overall sense of fulfilment.

At its core, journaling captures one's thoughts, feelings, and experiences on paper. The process involves translating the mind's inner workings into written words, creating a tangible record of one's journey through life. Reflective practices, intertwined with journaling, invite individuals to delve deeper into their experiences, examining the nuances of their emotions and thought patterns. The act of introspection, facilitated by journaling, bridges the conscious and subconscious, allowing individuals to navigate their inner landscape with greater clarity and understanding.

Journaling has several significant psychological advantages. Writing can be a therapeutic release for people, enabling them to process difficult situations, let go of unprocessed feelings and experience catharsis. This process of emotional expression contributes to stress reduction, providing a constructive and healthy means of coping with life's complexities. Moreover, journaling has been linked to improved mood regulation, increased self-awareness, and a greater sense of psychological well-being.

Journaling facilitates the cultivation of self-awareness—an essential component of emotional intelligence. Regularly engaging in reflective practices, individuals develop a heightened understanding of their emotions, triggers, and behavioral patterns. This self-awareness forms the foundation for more intentional decision-making, improved interpersonal relationships, and a deeper connection with one's authentic self. Journaling becomes a mirror that reflects the nuances of one's emotional landscape, fostering a conscious and intentional approach to navigating the complexities of life.

The structure of reflective journaling allows individuals to trace their personal growth and evolution over time. By revisiting past entries, individuals can observe development patterns, identify areas of resilience, and acknowledge moments of triumph or learning. This retrospective lens provides a valuable perspective on the journey of self-discovery, reinforcing the narrative of personal growth and resilience in the face of challenges. Journaling becomes a dynamic and living document—a testament to the ongoing process of becoming.

One of the distinctive aspects of journaling is its versatility in accommodating various styles and approaches. Some individuals prefer structured journaling, utilizing prompts or specific formats to guide their reflections. Others engage in free-form or stream-of-consciousness writing, allowing thoughts to flow organically onto the pages. Visual journaling, incorporating images, drawings, or collage elements, provides a creative outlet for those who resonate with graphic expression. The flexibility of journaling allows individuals to tailor their reflective practices to suit their unique preferences and needs.

The intersection of mindfulness and journaling creates a potent synergy that enhances the benefits of both practices. Mindful journaling involves approaching the act of writing with total presence and awareness. Individuals engage in the process with an open and non-judgmental mindset, observing their thoughts and emotions as they arise. This mindful approach deepens the reflective experience and cultivates a sense of acceptance and compassion toward oneself. Mindful journaling becomes a meditative practice—a moment of intentional connection with the present moment and the inner landscape.

Gratitude journaling represents a specialized form of reflective practice that focuses on acknowledging and expressing gratitude. This deliberate emphasis on the good aspects of life has been linked to various psychological advantages, such as elevated general wellbeing, elevated mood, and greater life satisfaction. Keeping a gratitude notebook helps you develop an appreciative mindset and a positive outlook on life by encouraging you to record your moments of thankfulness, small or large.

The therapeutic value of journaling is highlighted by its inclusion into therapeutic processes. Writing is a known therapeutic strategy used in journal therapy to help with self-examination, emotional release, and personal development. Journaling exercises are a common way for therapists to encourage clients to explore their ideas and feelings outside the therapeutic setting. This cooperative method strengthens the therapeutic bond and gives people the power to engage in rehabilitation actively.

Sharing one's innermost thoughts and experiences through writing can be a profoundly intimate and vulnerable process. While some individuals choose to keep their journals private, others may find value in sharing their reflections with trusted friends, family members, or support groups. This communal aspect of journaling creates a shared narrative of experiences, fostering connections and empathy among individuals who resonate with similar themes. The ability of shared stories to transcend personal experiences and foster a sense of the human journey's universality gives them their power.

Journalism g becomes particularly impactful during the transition, loss, or significant life changes. The reflective process provides a container for navigating the complexities of emotions during such times. Whether grappling with grief, embarking on a new chapter, or confronting unexpected challenges, journaling becomes a breakfast companion—a space to process, make meaning, and envision a path forward. Putting words to paper can be a beacon of self-discovery and resilience in times of uncertainty.

The digital age has ushered in new dimensions of journaling, with online platforms and digital tools offering alternative ways to engage in reflective practices. Blogging, digital journals, and mobile applications designed for reflective writing provide individuals with convenient and accessible avenues for self-expression. While the essence of journaling remains rooted in introspection, these digital mediums offer additional flexibility and convenience, catering to diverse preferences and lifestyles.

Despite the myriad benefits of journaling, potential barriers to consistent practice exist. Time constraints, perceived lack of writing skills, or the belief that one's thoughts are not significant enough to document are common obstacles. Overcoming these barriers involves reframing journaling as a flexible and accessible practice. Starting with small, manageable commitments, experimenting with different styles, and viewing journaling as a process rather than a product contribute to establishing a sustainable and enriching reflective practice.

In conclusion, journaling and reflective practices are gateways to the inner landscape—a journey of self-discovery, emotional expression, and personal growth. Whether through structured prompts, mindful exploration, or gratitude acknowledgment, journaling allows individuals to intentionally navigate their thoughts and emotions.

The psychological benefits of self-awareness, emotional regulation, and personal evolution underscore the transformative impact of journaling on overall well-being. As individuals engage in this intentional introspection, they embark on a dynamic and enriching exploration of their inner worlds, weaving a narrative of resilience, self-discovery, and the ongoing process of becoming.

CHAPTER VI

Creating a Calm Home Environment

Organizing and Decluttering

In the contemporary world, when our lives frequently follow a fast-paced rhythm, the places we live in significantly impact how our experiences and overall well-being are shaped. Organizing and decluttering has emerged as more than just a domestic task; it is a mindful and intentional approach to curating living spaces that foster harmony, efficiency, and a sense of tranquillity. Beyond, the mere arrangement of belongings, organizing, and decluttering becomes transformative, influencing the physical environment and individual's mental and emotional states. This section delves into the multifaceted aspects of organizing and decluttering, exploring the psychological benefits, practical strategies, and the profound impact these practices can have on creating spaces that nurture a sense of balance and well-being.

At its essence, organizing and decluttering involve the intentional arrangement and elimination of possessions within a space. The concept extends beyond mere tidying up; it encompasses a thoughtful evaluation of belongings, prioritization of essentials, and creation of systems that enhance functionality. Organizing is a dynamic process that evolves with changing needs and lifestyle, requiring a continuous commitment to maintaining order. When approached with mindfulness and intentionality, organizing and decluttering become powerful tools for transforming living spaces into sanctuaries that support the well-being of their inhabitants.

The psychological benefits of an organized and clutter-free environment are extensive. Studies have shown that the state of one's surroundings significantly impacts mental well-being, influencing factors such as stress levels, cognitive function, and emotional state. On the other hand, an organized space fosters a sense of control, clarity, and calmness, providing individuals with a supportive backdrop for their daily activities.

One of the central psychological benefits of organizing a decluttering is reducing stress. Clutter can create visual chaos, leading to a constant cognitive load as individuals navigate their living spaces. Decluttering simplifies the visual field, minimizing the stimuli that can increase stress levels. A cluttered environment promotes a sense of order, making it easier for individuals to focus, relax, and engage in activities without the mental distraction caused by disarray.

Moreover, an organized living space enhances cognitive function and productivity. The human brain is influenced by its surroundings, and clutter can cause cognitive overload, which impairs focus and judgment. In contrast, an organized and stress lined environment supports mental clarity, allowing individuals to think more clearly, make decisions more efficiently, and approach tasks with heightened focus and efficiency. This cognitive advantage extends to various aspects of life, from work-related activities to personal projects and daily routines.

The emotional impact of an organized and decluttered space is closely tied to well-being. Clutter has been associated with guilt, frustration, and feeling overwhelmed. Decluttering becomes a liberating process, allowing individuals to let go of possessions that no longer serve a purpose or hold emotional significance. Creating a curated and intentional space fosters a positive dynamic atmosphere, promoting feelings of contentment, satisfaction, and control of one's surroundings.

Organizing and decluttering extend beyond the physical environment; they influence lifestyle choices and consumption patterns. In a consumer-driven society, accumulation of possessions is often equated with success or happiness. However, intentional decluttering challenges this narrative, emphasizing the quality of possessions over quantity. This shift in perspective encourages mindful consumption, where individuals prioritize items that bring genuine joy, functionality, or significance into their lives. Decluttering becomes a conscious act of reevaluating one's relationship with material possessions and fostering a sense of gratitude for the items that genuinely enhance well-being.

Practical strategies for organizing and decluttering involve a systematic approach that considers individuals' unique needs and preferences. Marie Kondo's KonMari Method recommends decluttering based on whether an item "sparks joy." This strategy promotes a deliberate and thoughtful approach to decluttering by encouraging people to evaluate their belongings according to their emotional impact. Sorting possessions into categories and working on one at a time is another tactic that enables people to concentrate on particular sections of their homes and decide what to preserve, give away, or dispose of.

Decluttering can be emotionally charged, especially when it comes to sentimental items. Marie Kondo's approach emphasizes expressing gratitude for items before letting them go, recognizing their role in one's life. This mindful farewell acknowledges the emotional attachment while creating space for new experiences and memories, and, additionally, involving the entire household in organizing fosters a sense of shared responsibility. It ensures that the organizational systems put in place align with the needs and preferences of all residents.

Digital decluttering has become increasingly relevant in the age of technology. The digital landscape often mirrors the physical one, accumulating digital clutter in files, emails, and not fictions. Establishing digital organizational systems, regularly decluttering digital files, and curating online spaces contribute to a streamlined and efficient digital environment. Digital decluttering enhances productivity, reduces digital overwhelm, and fosters a healthier relationship with technology.

The concept of minimalism aligns closely with the principles of organizing and decluttering. Minimalism advocates simplifying one's life by focusing on essential possessions, eliminating excess, and prioritizing experiences over material accumulation. The minimalist approach challenges societal norms that equate happiness with the possession of more, encouraging individuals to redefine their values and priorities. A minimalist mindset contributes to a more intentional and conscious approach to organizing living spaces.

The impact of organizing and decluttering extends to various facets of life, including relationships and personal well-being. A cluttered and disorganized space can strain relationships, leading to conflict over shared spaces, difficulty finding belongings, and a general sense of chaos. Conversely, an organized and harmonious living space contributes to a positive atmosphere, facilitating open communication, shared responsibilities, and unity among household members. The benefits of a decluttered environment ripple through various aspects of life, fostering a sense of balance and well-being.

The benefits of organizing and decluttering are not limited to individual households; they extend to broader societal and environmental implications. Excessive consumption and waste contribute to ecological degradation, and a culture of mindful consumption aligns with sustainable living practices. Individuals who practice purposeful organizing and decluttering are part of a more significant movement to reduce waste, minimize environmental impact, and promote a more sustainable way of living.

In conclusion, organizing and decluttering represent more than superficial efforts to maintain a tidy living space; they encapsulate intentional and mindful practices that influence mental, emotional, and social well-being. The psychological benefits of reduced stress, enhanced cognitive function, and improved emotional well-being underscore the transformative impact of these practices. Whether adopting minimalist principles, embracing digital decluttering, or incorporating gratitude into the decluttering process, individuals can cultivate spaces that nurture a sense of harmony and balance. As we navigate the complexities of contemporary life, organizing and decluttering becomes a journey of self-discovery, reevaluating priorities, and a commitment to fostering well-being within our spaces.

Designating Relaxation Spaces

In modern life's fast-paced and demanding landscape, intentional relation spaces within our homes have gained recognition as a cornerstone of overall well-being. Designating specific areas dedicated to relaxation transcends mere aesthetics; it is a purposeful act of creating sanctuaries that promote tranquillity, mental rejuvenation, and a respite from the stresses of daily life. This section delves into the multifaceted aspects of designating relaxation spaces, exploring the psychological benefits, practical considerations, and the transformative impact these intentional environments can have on cultivating peace and balance in our lives.

At its core, designating relaxation spaces involves creating intentional pockets within our living environments, where the primary focus is on fostering calmness and rejuvenation. These spaces serve as retreats from the demands of work, family, and external pressures, offering individuals an opportunity to unwind, recharge, and engage in activities that promote mental and emotional well-being. The significance of relaxation spaces lies in their physical design and their psychological impact on individuals seeking solace and respite.

The psychological benefits of having designated relaxation spaces are profound and extend across various mental and emotional well-being aspects. In a world characterized by constant stimulation and digital connectivity, these spaces counterbalance by offering solitude and mindfulness. The intentional act of stepping into a relaxation space signals a shift in mindset, creating a mental boundary between the demands of the outside world and the internal need for rejuvenation. This mental separation fosters a sense of autonomy and control over one's well-being.

Stress reduction is one of the main psychological advantages of relaxation areas. A common feature of contemporary living is chronic stress, which is linked to a number of physical and mental health problems. Specialized areas for relaxation serve as safe havens where people can practice stress-relieving techniques like deep breathing, meditation, or just resting in a peaceful setting. These areas' purposeful design, which incorporates comfort and tranquillity rating features, adds to a sensory experience that helps reduce stress.

Moreover, relaxation spaces serve as catalysts from dullness—a practice linked to heightened awareness, improved focus, and a more profound connection with the present moment. Whether incorporating natural elements, soothing colors, or mindful activities like reading or journaling, these spaces become conducive to mindfulness practices. The intentional design elements, such as comfortable seating, soft lighting, and the exclusion of distractions, encourage individuals to immerse themselves fully in the present, fostering a mental state that transcends the rush of daily life.

Establishing purposeful areas for relaxing at home helps foster a healthy and encouraging mental atmosphere. These areas encourage people to put their mental and emotional health first by serving as reminders of the value of self-care. Setting up a designated space for resting conveys a strong message about how important one's mental health is, which supports a positive outlook and a sense of self-worth.

Practical considerations play a pivotal role in effectively designing and utilizing relaxation spaces. The location of these spaces within a home should align with the individual's preferences and lifestyle. Some may prefer secluded spaces away from high-traffic areas, while others may find comfort in integrating relaxation elements into shared living spaces. The design's flexibility allows for adapting these spaces to changing needs and preferences.

The selection of furniture, décor, and lighting dramatically influences the ambiance of leisure areas. Soft materials, plush cushions, and comfortable seating configurations enhance coziness and comfort. Natural components, like raw materials or plants, might improve the atmosphere's overall serenity by fostering a sense of connectedness to the outside world. Warm, gentle colors encourage relaxation, and artificial and natural lighting significantly establishes the mood.

Incorporating sensory elements into relaxation spaces enhances the overall experience. Aromatherapy can add a dimension of olfactory comfort through essential oils or scented candles. Soundscapes, whether through soft music, nature sounds, or white noise, contribute to a calming auditory environment. These sensory considerations contribute to a holistic approach, engaging multiple senses to create a harmonious and immersive relaxation experience.

The multifunctionality of relaxation spaces allows for diverse activities that cater to individual preferences. While some may find solace in meditative practices, others may prefer engaging in hobbies, reading, or listening to music. The key is creating a space that accommodates various activities, allowing individuals to tailor their relaxation experience based on their mood and needs at any time.

The digital age has introduced new dimensions to relaxation spaces, with technology influencing both the design and utilization of these environments. Incorporating smart home devices, such as programmable lighting or sound systems, allows for customizable and immersive experience. However, a delicate balance must be maintained to ensure that technology complements, rather than detracts from, the overall goal of creating a space for mental rejuvenation.

The transformative impact of relaxation spaces extends beyond the individual to influence interpersonal relationships and the overall atmosphere within a home. Shared relaxation spaces provide opportunities for connection and bonding among family members or cohabitants. Engaging in relaxation activities fosters a sense of unity, shared experiences, and open communication. The positive energy cultivated within these spaces ripples through the home, contributing to a harmonious and supportive living environment.

Designating relaxation spaces aligns with broader societal trends emphasizing the importance of holistic well-being. Integrating relaxation practices into daily life challenges the traditional dichotomy between work and leisure, encouraging individuals to view well-being as a continuous and integrated aspect of their lives. As workplaces increasingly adopt flexible and remote work arrangements, the need for intentional relaxation spas within homes becomes more pronounced, counterbalancing the blurring boundaries between professional and personal life.

In conclusion, the intentional act of de-igniting relaxation spaces within homes is a decisive step towards prioritizing mental and emotional well-being in the face of the demands of modern life. The psychological benefits, practical considerations, and transformative impact of these intentional environments contribute to a holistic approach to self-care. As individuals embrace the concept of creating actuaries for tranquillity, they embark on a journey of cultivating balance, mindfulness, and a profound connection with their well-being within the spaces they call home.

Establishing Routines and Boundaries
In the intricate dance of daily life, establishing routines and boundaries emerges as a foundational practice, offering individuals a compass to navigate the complexities of modern existence. These

intentional str lectures provide a framework for managing time, energy, and priorities, fostering a sense of order, predict ability, and balance. This section delves into the multifaceted dynamics of establishing routines and boundaries, exploring the psychological benefits, physical considerations, and the transformative impact these intentional practices can have on cultivating a life that aligns with individual values and aspirations.

At their essence, routines are patterns of behaviour or activities that follow a predictable sequence, providing a sense of structure and order to daily life. From morning to work routines and evening rituals, these patterns create a rhythm that helps individuals' transition between different phases of their day. The psychological benefits of routines are manifold, contributing to a sense of stability, reduced stress, and improved overall well-being.

One of the primary psychological benefits of establishing routines is reducing decision fatigue. In a world teeming with choices, the cognitive load of decision-making can be overwhelming. Routines automate certain aspects of daily life, allowing individuals to conserve mental energy for more critical decisions. By streamlining mundane tasks and activities, routines create a sense of efficiency, freeing up cognitive resources for more intentional and meaningful choices.

Moreover, routines provide a sense of predictability and control over one's environment. The human brain craves predictability and order, and routines offer a structured framework that instill a sense of security and familiarity. This predictability becomes especially crucial during times of uncertainty or stress, serving as a stabilizing force that individuals can rely on. The comfort derived from established routines contributes to emotional well-being, helping individuals navigate the uncertainties of life with greater resilience.

Establishing morning and evening routines bookends the day with intentional activities, influencing the overall trajectory of one's daily experience. Whether exercise, mindfulness practices, or nourishing activities, a morning routine becomes a launching pad for a day characterized by intentionality and purpose. Similarly, an evening routine signals a transition to relaxation and prepares the mind and body for restful sleep.

Routines play a crucial role in time management and goal attainment in work and productivity. Work routines, which may include specific start and end times, designated breaks, and structured task prioritization, contribute to increased productivity and more efficient use of time. By establishing a routine that aligns with individual work preferences and energy levels, individuals can optimize their workdays and reduce the likelihood of feeling overwhelmed or burnt out.

While routines provide a sense of structure and predict boundaries are protective barriers that define limits and delineate personal space and time. Establishing boundaries involves setting clear guidelines for acceptable behaviors, interactions, and commitments. The psychological benefits of boundaries are profound, contributing to improved mental health, increased self-esteem, and healthier interpersonal relationships.

In a hyperconnected world, individuals may be inundated with constant demands on time and attention. Setting boundaries allows individuals to protect their mental and emotional space, shielding them against external pressures and preventing burnout. This intentional practice becomes crucial in work-life balance, as clear boundaries help individuals navigate the delicate interplay between professional and personal responsibilities.

Furthermore, boundaries contribute to increased self-awareness and self-esteem. By clearly defining personal limits, decidual better understand their needs, values, and priorities. This self-awareness forms the foundation for healthy decision-making, as individuals can align their choices with their core values and aspirations. Setting and maintaining boundaries also communicates a sense of self-worth, reinforcing that personal well-being is a priority deserving of protection.

In interpersonal relationships, establishing boundaries fosters healthier and more respectful connections. Healthy boundaries ensure individuals engage in relationships based on mutual respect and consent, preventing the erosion of personal autonomy. Clearly communicated boundaries establish expectations, minimize miscommunications, and foster an atmosphere where people feel comfortable voicing their wants and preferences. Healthy boundaries allow people to interact authentically and with a sense of agency, fostering meaningful and fulfilling interactions.

Practical considerations play a crucial role in effectively establishing routines and boundaries. Aligning routines with individual preferences, circadian rhythms, and energy levels enhances sustainability. Flexibility within routines allows for adaptation to changing circumstances while maintaining the overall structure. Experimenting with different elements of routines, such as incorporating mindfulness practices or adjusting the sequence of activities, helps individuals tailor their routines to suit their unique needs and goals.

In the case of boundaries, effective communication is paramount. Articulating boundaries to others involves expression needs, expectations, and limits respectfully and assertively. Consistency in enforcing boundaries reinforces their legitimacy and communicates the importance of maintaining personal well-being. Creating physical and symbolic cues, such as designated workspaces or specific communication protocols, helps signal the presence of boundaries and supports their effective implementation.

The transformative impact of establishing routines and boundaries extends beyond the individual to influence broader societal and cultural norms. As individuals prioritize well-being through intentional practice, they contribute to a shift in societal values, challenging the glorification of constant busyness and promoting a more balanced and sustainable approach to life. Acknowledging the importance of routines and boundaries fosters cultures that prioritize employee well-being, increasing job satisfaction, productivity, and overall organizational health.

In conclusion, establishing routines and boundaries is a linchpin in pursuing a balanced and fulfilling life. The psychological benefits of routines, including reduced decision fatigue, increased predictable try, and improved time management, contribute to overall well-being. Similarly, establishing boundaries protects mental and emotional space, enhances self-awareness, and fosters healthier relationships. As individuals navigate the complexities of contemporary life, the intentional practices of routines and boundaries become guiding principles, shaping a life that aligns with individual values, priorities, and aspirations.

CHAPTER VII

Positive Discipline

Understanding Discipline vs. Punishment

Discipline and punishment are often used interchangeably, yet they represent distinct approaches with profound implications for shaping behavior and fostering personal development. Discipline, rooted in guidance, education, and positive reinforcement, aims to teach individuals self-control, responsibility, and a sense of morality. In contrast, punishment relies on coercion, fear, and the imposition of consequences to deter undesirable behavior. This section explores the nuanced differences between discipline and punishment, delving into the psychological implications, the impact on character development, and the role these approaches play in cultivating positive behavior and well-rounded individuals.

When viewed through a positive lens, discipline embodies a holistic approach to behavior management that prioritizes understanding, guidance, and education. The etymology of the word "discipline" traces back to the Latin word "discipline," which means teaching, learning, and knowledge. Discipline seeks to instill values, cultivate self-control, and guide individuals toward responsible decision-making. Positive discipline recognizes the developmental stages of individuals, acknowledging that the learning process involves making mistakes and understanding the consequences of actions.

Positive discipline emphasizes setting clear expectations and boundaries while fostering open communication. It involves teaching individuals the principles of empathy, respect, and responsibility. When faced with undesirable behavior, the focus is on understanding and addressing the underlying causes constructively. Positive discipline strategies include active listening, problem-solving, and collaborative decision-making, encouraging individuals to internalize the values and principles taught.

Crucially, positive discipline places a strong emphasis on positive reinforcement. Acknowledging and rewarding positive behavior motivates individuals to repeat actions that align with societal norms and expectations. This approach capitalizes on the psychological principle of operant conditioning, where positive outcomes reinforce desired behavior. Positive discipline strategies, such as praise, encouragement, and rewards, create a supportive environment that nurtures a sense of self-worth and fosters intrinsic motivation.

In contrast, punishment operates on the premise of deterring undesirable behavior through imposition of negative consequences. The focus is on external control, often involving punitive measures such as time-outs, loss of privileges, or physical consequences. The roots of punishment are embedded in the idea of retribution, seeking to inflict discomfort or pain as a response to unacceptable behavior. While punishment may suppress behavior temporarily, it does not inherently teach individuals the values or skills needed for long-term behavior modification.

One of the primary criticisms of punishment is its potential to generate adverse side effects. The fear associated with punishment may lead to resentment, defiance, or a focus on avoiding punishment rather than internalizing positive values. Moreover, punishment may fail to address the underlying causes of behavior, merely suppressing symptoms without addressing the root issues. The coercive nature of punishment can strain relationships, creating an atmosphere of hostility or fear rather than one of mutual understanding and trust.

The psychological impact of discipline and punishment on character development is substantial and enduring. As a positive and educational approach, discipline contributes to developing individuals with strong moral compasses, a sense of responsibility, and intrinsic motivation. Positive discipline cultivates a growth mindset, in which people view obstacles as chances for growth and development. Positive discipline that strongly emphasizes empathy and understanding develops emotionally competent people who can behave with kindness and respect in social circumstances.

On the other hand, punishment could have unforeseen effects on a person's character development. Punitive measures can cause feelings of inadequacy, hostility, or a distorted perception of authority due to the fear and anxiety they engender. Punished people may internalize a sense of helplessness, which impedes the growth of autonomy and self-control. Avoiding bad outcomes at the expense of internalizing good values might lead to shallow conformity to social norms without properly comprehending their importance.

The long-term implications of discipline and punishment are evident in various aspects of an individual's life. Positive discipline forms individuals who exhibit self-control, resilience, and a sense of responsibility. These individuals are more likely to engage in prosocial behavior, contribute positively to their communities, and navigate challenges with a constructive mindset. The positive reinforcement and guidance received during childhood through positive discipline lay the foundation for healthy interpersonal relationships and a well-rounded approach to life.

On the contrary, the effects of punishment may manifest in maladaptive behaviors, including defiance, aggression, or fear-driven compliance. Individuals who have experienced punitive measures may struggle with trust issues, exhibit externalized behavior problems, or develop negative attitudes toward authority figures. The punishment strategy, which emphasizes outside control, may impede the growth of critical life skills, including emotional control, conflict resolution, and problem-solving.

The role of discipline and punishment extends beyond individual development to societal structures and cultural norms. In educational settings, the choice between positive discipline and punishment shapes the learning environment and influences the relationships between educators and students. Positive discipline in education promotes a collaborative and supportive atmosphere where educators act as mentors, guiding students toward personal growth and academic success. This approach fosters a love of learning, intrinsic motivation, and a positive school culture.

In contrast, punitive measures in education may contribute to a climate of fear, compliance, or rebellion. The emphasis on control through punishment can create a hierarchical dynamic that hinders open communication and collaboration. The punitive approach might not address the underlying reasons for behavioral problems or academic difficulties, continuing a vicious cycle of negative reinforcement without providing opportunities for personal growth and development.

Understanding the role of discipline and punishment is especially critical in the context of criminal justice systems. The traditional punitive approach, focused on punishment as retribution, has come under scrutiny for its limited effectiveness in reducing recidivism and rehabilitating individuals. Alternatives such as restorative justice, which emphasizes accountability, empathy, and repairing harm, align more closely with the principles of positive discipline. Restorative justice addresses the root causes of criminal behavior, promotes healing for victims, and reintegrating offenders into society as responsible and empathetic individuals.

In contemporary parenting, the choice between discipline and punishment profoundly influences the parent-child relationship and the development of essential life skills. Emotionally intelligent and resilient people are developed through natural consequences, choices, and clear expectations—all of which are components of positive disciplinary techniques. The development of a solid parent-child bond, communication, and understanding are given top priority by parents who use positive discipline techniques.

Conversely, relying on punishment in parenting may strain the parent-child relationship, leading to power struggles, resentment, or fear-driven compliance. Punitive measures such as corporal punishment have been associated with adverse outcomes, including increased aggression, antisocial behavior, and mental health issues in children. The shift towards positive discipline in parenting aligns with evolving societal values, recognizing the importance of nurturing emotionally healthy and socially responsible individuals.

In conclusion, the nuances between discipline and punishment encompass profound implications for individual development, character formation, and societal structures. When approached positively, discipline is an educational tool that fosters intrinsic motivation, responsibility, and moral development. Positive discipline emphasizes understanding, guidance, and the cultivation of essential life skills. In contrast, punishment relies on external control, fear, and coercion to deter undesirable behavior, often leading to unintended consequences.

The choice between discipline and punishment extends to various facets of life, including education, criminal justice, and parenting. Embracing positive discipline creates individuals who exhibit resilience, emotional intelligence, and a sense of responsibility. In contrast, the punitive approach may yield short-term compliance but risks hindering the development of autonomy, self-regulation, and a genuine understanding of societal values. As societies evolve, the emphasis on positive discipline becomes integral to cultivating well-rounded individuals who contribute positively to their communities and navigate life's challenges with a constructive and empathetic mindset.

Implementing Positive Reinforcement

Positive reinforcement, rooted in behavioral psychology, is a powerful and practical approach to shaping behavior and fostering personal development. Unlike punitive measures or strict discipline, positive reinforcement encourages desired behavior by introducing rewards or positive stimuli. This section explores the principles and applications of positive reinforcement, delving into the psychological mechanisms at play, the impact on individual motivation, and how this approach can be implemented across various contexts to create a positive and supportive environment.

At its core, positive reinforcement operates on the principle of strengthening behavior by associating it with a positive outcome. This psychological mechanism is grounded in the work of B.F. A renowned psychologist and behaviorist, Skinner demonstrated that behavior followed by a rewarding consequence is likely to be repeated. In positive reinforcement, rewards can take various forms, including verbal praise, tangible rewards, or opportunities for preferred activities. The key is to create a connection between the behavior and a positive outcome, motivating individuals to engage in the desired behavior more frequently.

Positive reinforcement's psychological underpinnings align with operant conditioning principles, a form of learning where behavior is influenced by its consequences. Positive reinforcement involves presenting a stimulus (the reward) immediately after a behavior occurs, increasing the likelihood that the behavior will be repeated. The immediacy and consistency of the reinforcement play crucial roles in establishing the association between the behavior and the reward.

The capacity of positive reinforcement to increase intrinsic motivation is one of its core features. In contrast to external control strategies like punishment, which rely on intimidation or force, positive reinforcement appeals to people's inner motivations and goals. Individuals are more likely to feel a sense of autonomy, contentment, and accomplishment when their activity results in positive outcomes. When individuals experience positive outcomes due to their behavior, they are more likely to feel a sense of accomplishment, autonomy, and satisfaction. This internal sense of reward fosters intrinsic motivation, where individuals engage in the desired behavior because they find it inherently fulfilling and enjoyable.

Positive reinforcement impacts people's attitudes, self-perception, and general well-being in addition to the immediate behavioral changes. Verbal praise conveys acceptance, acknowledgment, and a sense of value while acknowledging a particular behavior. Positive reinforcement contributes to developing a positive self-concept, reinforcing the idea that individuals are capable, worthy of recognition, and capable of contributing positively to their environment.

In educational settings, implementing positive reinforcement has gained recognition as a powerful tool for promoting student engagement, motivation, and academic success. Teachers who incorporate positive reinforcement strategies create a classroom environment that values effort, perseverance, and a growth mindset. By providing timely and specific feedback, recognizing achievements, and offering incentives, educators empower students to take an active role in their learning journey.

Tangible rewards, such as stickers or certificates, serve as concrete representations of accomplishment, reinforcing the positive connection between effort and success. Moreover, when delivered sincerely and precisely, verbal praise communicates to students that their contributions are seen, valued, and appreciated. Positive reinforcement in education motivates students to excel academically and fosters a love for learning and a sense of self-efficacy.

Positive reinforcement is instrumental in promoting a positive organizational culture, boosting morale, and enhancing employee performance in the workplace. Leaders who actively recognize and reward employees for their contributions create a motivating work environment. Recognition programs, employee-of-the-month awards, or verbal praise during team meetings are tools for acknowledging individual and collective achievements.

Positive reinforcement significantly impacts employee retention, satisfaction, and overall organizational success in the workplace. Workers are likely to be engaged, devoted, and inspired to put forth their best efforts if they feel valued and appreciated. Positive reinforcement contributes to a positive feedback loop, where employees are encouraged to continue exhibiting desired behaviors, leading to improved individual and team performance.

Positive reinforcement is a cornerstone of effective discipline and behavior management in parenting. Parents who use positive reinforcement techniques create a nurturing and supportive family environment. Verbal praise, encouragement, and a reward system can be powerful tools for reinforcing positive behavior in children. The consistency of positive reinforcement helps children understand expectations, develop a sense of responsibility, and internalize values and social norms.

Implementing positive reinforcement in parenting involves being specific about the behavior being reinforced, providing timely feedback, and ensuring that the rewards are meaningful to the child. Using a reward chart, where children earn stars or tokens for completing tasks or exhibiting positive behavior, is a popular and practical positive reinforcement strategy. This motivates children to engage in desired behaviors and teaches them the concept of earning rewards through effort and responsibility.

Positive reinforcement is crucial in achieving goals and cultivating positive habits in personal development and habit formation. Positive reinforcement can be a powerful motivator, whether striving for fitness goals, adopting healthier lifestyle choices, or building new skills. Acknowledging small victories, celebrating milestones, and incorporating rewards into the process create a positive feedback loop that sustains motivation and momentum.

Setting defined goals, breaking them down into doable steps, and establishing clear rewards for reaching each milestone are all part of implementing positive reinforcement in personal growth. By linking positive outcomes to desired behaviors, individuals create a sense of accountability and motivation that propels them toward their objectives. The positive reinforcement approach promotes a growth mindset, resilience, and an optimistic outlook on personal development.

While positive reinforcement is a valuable and effective strategy, its successful implementation requires careful consideration and individualization. The choice of rewards should align with the preferences and values of the individuals involved. What may be reinforcing for one person may not have the same impact on another. Additionally, the timing of reinforcement is critical, with immediate feedback enhancing the association between behavior and reward.

Furthermore, the concept of shaping, a technique derived from operant conditioning, involves reinforcing successive approximations of the desired behavior. This gradual reinforcement of behaviors that move closer to the target behavior allows for a step-by-step approach to behavior modification. Shaping is particularly effective when working towards complex or long-term goals, allowing individuals to build towards the desired behavior in manageable increments.

While positive reinforcement is a powerful tool, it is essential to acknowledge that it is not a one-size-fits-all solution. Some individuals may respond more positively to certain types of reinforcement than others. Additionally, overreliance on extrinsic rewards without fostering intrinsic motivation may diminish the effectiveness of positive reinforcement over time. Therefore, a balanced approach incorporating various reinforcement strategies is often the most effective in creating lasting behavior change.

In conclusion, positive reinforcement is a versatile and impactful approach to shaping behavior, fostering motivation, and promoting personal development. Positive reinforcement, rooted in operant conditioning, associates behavior with favorable results to encourage repeating that action. Positive reinforcement contributes to a positive and supportive environment that nurtures intrinsic motivation, resilience, and a growth mindset, whether applied in education, the workplace, parenting, or personal development. As individuals and organizations recognize the power of positive reinforcement, they unlock the potential for sustained behavioral change, personal growth, and creating positive and thriving communities.

Consistency in Parenting

Consistency in parenting is a fundamental principle that shapes the parent-child relationship and profoundly influences a child's emotional well-being and development. It entails maintaining a stable and predictable environment where expectations, rules, and responses to behavior remain uniform over time. This section explores the significance of consistency in parenting, delving into the psychological implications, the impact on child development, and practical strategies for fostering a consistent and supportive parenting approach.

At its core, consistency in parenting provides a sense of security and predictability for children. A child's developing brain thrives on routine and structure, and consistency serves as the scaffolding upon which healthy development unfolds. When children know what to expect in their environment, they feel a sense of safety, which is crucial for forming secure attachments and developing a positive self-concept.

Consistency is evident in various aspects of parenting, including setting and enforcing rules, establishing routines, and responding to behaviors. When parents are consistent in their expectations and consequences for behavior, children learn about boundaries, develop a sense of responsibility, and internalize values that guide their decision-making. Encouraging children to comprehend the repercussions of their actions through consistent discipline helps them develop empathy and self-control.

On the other hand, inconsistent parenting can lead to confusion and insecurity in children. When rules are arbitrary, or enforcement varies depending on the parent's mood or circumstances, children may struggle to understand the boundaries of acceptable behavior. Inconsistency in responses to behavior can create uncertainty, leaving children feeling anxious or frustrated. This lack of predictability can impact a child's emotional regulation, making navigating social situations and forming healthy relationships challenging.

One of the primary psychological benefits of consistency in parenting is establishing trust between parent and child. Trust is a foundational element in any healthy relationship and is particularly crucial in the parent-child dynamic. When children trust that their parents' responses will be consistent and fair, they develop a secure attachment, a vital component for emotional well-being and healthy social development.

Consistent parenting helps build a sense of reliability and dependability in the parent-child relationship. Children who experience consistency in their caregivers are more likely to feel secure in seeking comfort, expressing emotions, and exploring their environment. The secure attachment formed through consistent parenting becomes a psychological anchor that supports the child's emotional resilience and adaptability to life's challenges.

In discipline, consistency is a linchpin for effective behavior management. When consequences for behavior are consistently applied, children learn to associate specific actions with predictable outcomes. This clarity helps children understand the principles of cause and effect, facilitating the development of a sense of responsibility and accountability for their actions. Consistent discipline also communicates to children that rules are not arbitrary but are designed to ensure their safety, well-being, and social competence.

Moreover, consistent responses to behavior contribute to children's emotional regulation development. Children internalize these skills when parents consistently model and teach healthy emotional expression and coping strategies. Consistency in providing emotional support and guidance helps children learn to navigate their emotions effectively, promoting resilience and adaptive coping mechanisms.

Practical consistency in parenting involves clear communication of expectations and consequences. Parents should articulate rules and expectations age-appropriately and align with the child's developmental stage. Consistent rules provide children with a framework for understanding the boundaries of acceptable behavior and contribute to a harmonious family environment.

Consistency extends to the enforcement of consequences for behavior. When consequences are applied consistently, children learn that their actions have predictable outcomes. This predictability is essential for the development of cause-and-effect thinking and the understanding of social norms. Consistent consequences also contribute to fairness, as all children are treated equitably, fostering a sense of justice and equality within the family unit.

In routines, consistency is crucial in creating a structured and stable environment. Daily routines, such as mealtimes, bedtimes, and homework schedules, give children a sense of order and predictability. Consistent routines help develop time-management skills, regulate sleep patterns, and create opportunities for positive parent-child interactions.

Consistency in routines is particularly beneficial during times of transition or stress. During challenging periods, such as moving to a new home or adjusting to a new school, consistent routines act as anchors, providing children with a familiar and secure framework.

Routines become a source of comfort and stability, helping children navigate change with greater resilience.

While consistency is a cornerstone of effective parenting, it is essential to acknowledge that it does not imply rigidity or inflexibility. Flexibility within consistent parenting allows for adjustments based on individual needs, developmental stages, or specific circumstances. Consistent parenting involves balancing firmness with warmth and providing children with structure while allowing age-appropriate autonomy and exploration.

Inconsistent parenting patterns can emerge for various reasons, including stress, exhaustion, or a lack of awareness of the importance of consistency. Parents may find themselves inconsistently enforcing rules, responding differently to similar behaviors, or varying routines haphazardly. Establishing a steady and nurturing atmosphere for kids requires identifying and resolving erratic behaviors.

Self-awareness and introspection on the part of parents are essential to teaching consistency. Periodically assessing their parenting style and pinpointing areas where consistency needs to be reinforced can benefit parents. Consulting parental resources, neighbourhood groups, or expert advice can offer helpful perspectives and techniques for overcoming obstacles consistently.

In conclusion, consistency in parenting is a dynamic and essential principle that contributes to children's emotional well-being and development. It provides a stable and predictable environment, fostering secure attachments, trust, and a positive self-concept.

Consistency in setting and enforcing rules, establishing routines, and responding to behavior contributes to effective behavior management, developing emotional regulation, and cultivating responsibility in children. Parents who actively incorporate consistency into their parenting style and understand its importance foster a loving and supportive home environment that promotes the healthy growth of children.

CHAPTER VIII

Parental Self-Care

Importance of Self-Care for Parents

The journey of parenthood is a profound and rewarding experience marked by love, joy, and the fulfilment of nurturing a new life. However, amidst the joys and responsibilities, parents often face significant challenges and demands that can impact their physical, emotional, and mental well-being. While caring for their children, parents must recognize the importance of self-care. Self-care for parents goes beyond mere indulgence; it is a vital aspect of maintaining one's overall health, preserving a sense of identity, and building resilience in the face of the complexities of parenthood.

Parenthood, with its myriad responsibilities, can lead to the neglect of parents' well-being. The demanding nature of caring for a child, managing household tasks, and, in many cases, balancing a career can result in exhaustion and burnout. Self-care is a deliberate and proactive approach to maintaining physical and mental health, ensuring that parents are better equipped to handle their challenges and provide optimal care for their children.

Physical well-being is a cornerstone of effective parenting, and self-care plays a central role in preserving and enhancing it. The demands of caring for a child, especially in the early years, can be physically taxing. Sleep deprivation, irregular eating patterns, and a lack of exercise are common challenges that parents face. Prioritizing self-care through adequate sleep, balanced nutrition, and regular physical activity is essential for parents to maintain their energy levels, cognitive function, and overall health.

For parents, in particular, getting enough sleep is essential since it directly affects their capacity to handle the responsibilities of parenthood. In addition to impairing emotional and cognitive abilities, sleep deprivation lowers immunity, which puts parents at higher risk of sickness. Self-care techniques that promote improved physical and emotional resilience include creating a sleep-friendly atmosphere, establishing good sleep habits, and rotating evening tasks.

Another essential part of parent self-care is a balanced diet. Being a parent frequently results in erratic eating habits or a dependence on convenience foods, which may be deficient in essential nutrients. Making a healthy diet a priority gives parents the energy and nutrition they need to fulfil the responsibilities of parenthood. Preparing meals, including a range of fruits and vegetables, and drinking plenty of water are doable actions that contribute to physical well-being.

Regular physical activity contributes to physical health and positively affects mental and emotional well-being. Exercise releases endorphins, the body's natural mood enhancers, reducing stress and promoting well-being. Parents can incorporate physical activity into their routine by choosing activities they enjoy, such as walking, cycling, or participating in fitness classes. Moreover, involving children in physical activities fosters a healthy lifestyle for the entire family.

Emotional well-being is intricately connected to self-care, and acknowledging and addressing emotions is crucial to parental self-care. The emotional demands of parenthood, coupled with societal expectations and the desire to be a perfect parent, can lead to stress, anxiety, and feelings of inadequacy. Self-care involves recognizing and validating one's emotions, seeking support when needed, and implementing strategies to manage stress.

Regular self-reflection is an essential self-care technique that helps parents recognize and manage their feelings. Parents can discover sources of stress, get insights into their moods, and create coping mechanisms by journaling, practicing mindfulness, or just spending some quiet time introspecting. Setting reasonable goals, admitting flaws, and realizing it's acceptable to seek assistance when necessary are further components of emotional self-care.

Seeking support is a vital aspect of emotional self-care. Parenthood does not come with a manual, and every parent faces unique challenges. Connecting with other parents, joining support groups, or seeking professional help when necessary provides a valuable network for sharing experiences, gaining insights, and receiving emotional support. Establishing open communication with a partner, family members, or friends creates a supportive environment where parents feel heard and understood.

Mental well-being is closely intertwined with emotional health; self-care practices promoting mental well-being are essential for parents. The constant juggling of responsibilities, decision-making, and adapting to a child's changing needs can be mentally draining. Mindfulness and relaxation techniques are effective self-care strategies that enhance mental well-being.

Being mindful entails paying attention to thoughts and feelings without passing judgment on them and being in the present moment. Including mindfulness exercises like yoga, meditation, or deep breathing in everyday tasks gives parents peace and clarity. These techniques lessen stress and enhance focus, judgment, and cognitive performance.

One of the most important parts of mental self-care is setting limits. Parents may feel overcommitted and overextended due to the many demands on their time and attention during parenthood. Setting up unambiguous boundaries about time and personal space enables parents to put their health first and avoid burnout. Three critical tactics for preserving mental health include setting aside time for self-care, assigning responsibilities, and learning when to say no.

Preserving a sense of identity is a significant challenge for many parents, as the focus often shifts entirely to the child's needs. Self-care involves recognizing and nurturing one's interests, passions, and goals. Maintaining a sense of identity contributes to personal fulfillment and sets a positive example for children, emphasizing the importance of pursuing one's aspirations.

Maintaining social relationships outside of motherhood, following personal interests, and taking up hobbies all contribute to a well-rounded sense of self. Setting aside time for enjoyable and fulfilling pursuits keeps parents linked to their unique selves and promotes a healthy balance between parenting responsibilities and personal pleasure. Engaging kids in group activities also helps them feel connected and appreciate each other's company.

Balancing parenting responsibilities with personal and professional demands requires effective time management, another critical aspect of self-care. Prioritizing and organizing tasks, setting realistic goals, and recognizing the value of downtime contribute to an effective time-management strategy. Allocating time for self-care activities, whether exercise, reading, or pursuing a hobby, ensures that parents prioritize their well-being amidst their numerous responsibilities.

The importance of self-care for parents extends beyond individual well-being to the overall dynamics of the family. A parent who practices self-care is better equipped to handle parenting challenges, maintain a positive and supportive family environment, and model healthy behaviors for their children. Children benefit from observing parents who prioritize self-care and learning valuable lessons about the importance of well-being, balance, and self-respect.

In conclusion, self-care is an integral aspect of effective parenting, contributing to parents' overall health and well-being. Physical, emotional, and mental well-being are interconnected components that require intentional and consistent attention. By prioritizing self-care, parents enhance their ability to navigate the complexities of parenthood and set the stage for a positive and nurturing family environment. Acknowledging the value of self-care is an essential component of resilient and ethical parenting, not a self-serving gesture. Parenting that prioritizes their health creates the foundation for a happier, healthier, and more fulfilling family life.

Finding Time for Personal Hobbies

In the hustle and bustle of daily life, filled with professional responsibilities, family obligations, and the constant buzz of technology, finding time for personal hobbies can often seem like a luxury reserved for rare leisure moments. However, pursuing personal hobbies is not merely a frivolous indulgence but a vital aspect of self-care and personal growth. This section explores the significance of personal hobbies, the challenges of carving out time for them in a busy world, and the benefits individuals reap when they prioritize and cultivate their passions.

Personal hobbies encompass diverse activities that individuals engage in for enjoyment, relaxation, and personal fulfillment. From artistic pursuits like painting and playing musical instruments to physical activities like gardening or sports, hobbies provide an avenue for expressing creativity, relieving stress and fostering a sense of accomplishment. While the specific hobbies may vary widely among individuals, the common thread is the intrinsic joy and satisfaction derived from these activities.

One of the primary challenges individuals face in finding time for personal hobbies is the relentless pace of modern life. The demands of work, family, and social commitments often leave individuals feeling stretched thin, with little room for activities that may seem non-essential. The perception of personal hobbies as 'extra' or 'optional' often relegates them to the bottom of the priority list, resulting in neglected passions and unexplored interests.

Finding time for personal hobbies has become more difficult in the digital age despite its incredible convenience and connectedness. People may experience time scarcity and feel overwhelmed due to the constant onslaught of emails and notifications and the desire to browse social media. Scheduling specific time for hobbies is made more challenging by the fuzziness of the lines separating work and personal life.

Nevertheless, despite these difficulties, making time for personal interests is crucial. People are happier and more fulfilled when they participate in joyful activities. Engaging in hobbies is a potent way for people to detach from the stresses of everyday life and lose themselves in pursuits they are enthusiastic about.

Personal hobbies also play a crucial role in promoting mental health. The immersive nature of engaging in a hobby, whether reading, painting, or gardening, allows individuals to enter a state of flow. In this mental state, they are fully absorbed in the activity, experiencing deep concentration and a sense of timelessness. This flow state has been linked to increased happiness, reduced anxiety, and enhanced overall well-being.

Furthermore, personal hobbies contribute to developing a well-rounded and balanced life. In pursuing career success or fulfilling familial responsibilities, individuals may unintentionally neglect other dimensions of their identity. Hobbies provide an avenue for self-expression, exploration, and developing skills and interests outside the scope of professional or familial roles. This multifaceted engagement with life contributes to a sense of wholeness and personal fulfillment.

Carving out time for personal hobbies is not selfish but an investment in one's physical and emotional well-being. The rejuvenating effects of engaging in a hobby extend beyond the duration of the activity itself. Individuals who prioritize their passions often find themselves more energized, focused, and resilient in facing the challenges of daily life. The benefits of a well-nurtured hobby reverberate through various aspects of an individual's life, positively impacting relationships, work performance, and overall life satisfaction.

Despite the myriad benefits, individuals often need help with the practicalities of finding time for personal hobbies. A first step towards prioritizing hobbies involves a mindset shift recognizing the importance of self-care and personal fulfillment. Acknowledging that emotional well-being is a priority and not an afterthought sets the foundation for actively seeking and creating opportunities for hobby engagement.

Finding time for personal activities requires effective time management. People can begin by assessing their weekly or daily schedules and pinpointing certain times to set aside for their interests.

This may designate particular times, like an hour on the weekend morning or an hour in the evening, just for your activity. Making personal hobbies a regular part of one's routine requires conscious scheduling and commitment to this time.

Setting reasonable expectations is another crucial component of incorporating personal activities into a busy schedule. Understanding that extended hobby participation may not be possible daily and that occasional setbacks are normal might help people deal with prospective setbacks without giving up. Being adaptable in your approach relieves pressure to follow a strict plan in the face of changing circumstances.

Prioritizing personal hobbies may also involve negotiating boundaries with external demands. Communicating one's need for dedicated hobby time with family members or colleagues' fosters understanding and support. Establishing clear boundaries, such as designating specific hours as 'hobby time' and minimizing distractions during this period, helps create an environment conducive to focused engagement.

Digital detox is an increasingly popular strategy for finding time for personal hobbies and unplugging from electronic devices, even for a short duration. It can free up time that would otherwise be spent mindlessly scrolling or responding to work emails. Creating a designated 'tech-free' zone during hobby time enhances the immersive and therapeutic aspects of the activity.

Including personal interests in everyday activities is another good strategy to guarantee constant participation. People can, for instance, integrate their hobbies with their current activities by, for example, combining physical activities like walking or cycling into their workout regimen or listening to audiobooks or podcasts on their interests while commuting.

Another factor in integrating personal hobbies into daily life is their social component. Participating in organizations, hobby groups, or schools offers a social and structured setting that improves accountability and motivation. Engaging in hobbies as a group endeavor and as chances for bonding are created when shared experiences are had with friends or family.

Furthermore, the advantages of having a personal hobby extend beyond leisure time. Businesses and organizations are increasingly realizing the benefits of hobbies on workers' productivity and well-being. Employees who work in an atmosphere that supports work-life balance and lets them pursue their passions are happier and more engaged.

In conclusion, finding time for personal hobbies is not an indulgence but a vital component of maintaining overall well-being in contemporary life's fast-paced and demanding landscape. Recognizing the significance of personal passions, cultivating a mindset that prioritizes self-care, and implementing practical strategies for time management are essential steps in ensuring that personal hobbies become an integral and consistent part of daily life. As individuals actively engage with their passions, they experience the immediate benefits of stress relief and joy and contribute to a balanced, fulfilling, and enriched life.

Seeking Support from Others

In the intricate tapestry of human experience, the journey through life is marked by various challenges, triumphs, and moments that shape our narratives. Amidst the complexity of this journey, seeking support from others emerges as a powerful and essential aspect of navigating the inevitable ups and downs. This section explores the significance of seeking support, its various forms, and its transformative impact on individuals' well-being, resilience, and sense of connection.

At its core, seeking support is an acknowledgment of human vulnerability and an embrace of the inherent interdependence that characterizes human existence. As people realize that asking for help is not a sign of weakness but instead of strength and knowledge, the myth of self-sufficiency is disproved. Reaching out to others for support, whether in the face of stress, personal struggles, or accomplishments, builds a network of connections that enhances the human experience.

One of the primary forms of support is emotional support, which involves sharing one's feelings, experiences, and vulnerabilities with trusted individuals. This support is foundational for emotional well-being, providing a safe space for individuals to express themselves authentically. Emotional support fosters a sense of validation, empathy, and understanding, creating a buffer against feelings of isolation or loneliness. Talking through challenges or joys with a friend, family member, or confidant can be profoundly therapeutic, offering a fresh perspective and alleviating the emotional burden.

Practical support is another vital dimension of seeking assistance from others. In times of tangible challenges or overwhelming tasks, practical support may involve assistance with daily responsibilities, such as childcare, household chores, or logistical arrangements. Friends, family, or community members can step in to share the load, providing relief and creating a sense of collective responsibility. This form of support is particularly crucial during life transitions, crises, or periods of increased stress when the demands on an individual's time and energy may exceed their capacity.

The corollary to practical support is instrumental, which entails getting material resources, counsel, or direction. Whether money, expert counsel, or specialized knowledge, instrumental support gives people the resources and tools they need to overcome obstacles. Making educated judgments, conquering challenges, and accomplishing personal or professional goals can all be facilitated by seeking advice from mentors, professionals, or informed peers.

The power of asking for help is particularly pronounced when it comes to mental health. Problems with mental health, such as stress, depression, or anxiety, can have a significant effect on someone's quality of life and general well-being. One of the most critical steps on the road to recovery and healing is to seek assistance from mental health specialists like therapists or counselors. These experts provide specialized assistance, coping mechanisms, therapeutic interventions, and a secure environment where people can explore their feelings. Seeking help is normalized in a culture that de-stigmatizes mental health support and promotes candid discussions about mental health.

The importance of seeking support extends beyond individual well-being to the dynamics of relationships and communities. The willingness to seek and offer support creates a reciprocal and dynamic exchange in interpersonal relationships. Friends, family members, and partners who actively support each other contribute to developing trusting and resilient relationships. This mutual support fosters a sense of belonging, security, and shared growth, enhancing the overall quality of relationships.

Communities are vital in providing support networks defined by geographic proximity, shared interests, or everyday experiences. Community support can manifest in various forms, from neighbourhood assistance during crises to online forums connecting individuals with shared experiences. A community's sense of belonging and shared identity creates a support system that transcends individual challenges, emphasizing collective strength and resilience.

Although asking for help can be a very effective tool, it also necessitates being open to receiving it and willing to be vulnerable. Social pressures to be independent and self-sufficient make it difficult for people to ask for help because they worry about being judged or think doing so is a show of weakness. It helps to create situations where people feel secure and encouraged to reach out when cultural narratives are shifted to embrace the idea that asking for help is a daring and adaptable behavior.

Moreover, cultural and systemic factors can impact individuals' access to support. The stigma surrounding mental health, limited resources for specific communities, or systemic barriers to accessing professional help can hinder individuals from seeking the support they need. Addressing these disparities requires collective efforts to promote inclusivity, reduce stigma, and ensure that support systems are accessible to all individuals, regardless of their background or circumstances.

The transformative impact of seeking support is evident in numerous real-life stories where individuals facing adversity have found strength and resilience through connection. Shared experiences of overcoming challenges, whether personal, professional, or societal, underscore the profound impact of support networks. Support can come from unexpected places, emphasizing the importance of remaining open to connection and recognizing that individuals do not have to navigate their journeys alone.

In conclusion, seeking support from others is a dynamic and multifaceted aspect of the human experience that profoundly influences individual well-being, relationships, and communities. Whether in times of celebration or adversity, reaching out to others creates a tapestry of connection that enriches and strengthens the fabric of our lives. Emotional, practical, and instrumental support form a continuum that addresses various dimensions of human need, contributing to resilience, growth, and a sense of shared humanity.

By fostering a culture that values and normalizes seeking support, individuals, communities, and societies can create environments where everyone feels empowered to navigate life's challenges with the strength of connection.

CHAPTER IX

Parenting as a Team

Effective Co-Parenting Strategies

Co-parenting, the collaborative effort between separated or divorced parents to raise their children, is a complex and delicate undertaking that significantly influences the well-being and development of the children involved. While the end of a romantic relationship may mark the conclusion of a partnership, the responsibilities of parenting endure. Effective co-parenting involves navigating shared decision-making, communication, and mutual respect to provide a stable and supportive environment for children. This section explores the critical components of effective co-parenting, the challenges it may present, and strategies to foster positive parental partnerships that prioritize the children's best interests.

Effective co-parenting starts with communication. A cooperative and harmonious co-parenting relationship is based on establishing open and honest communication channels between co-parents. Establishing and maintaining a regular and transparent line of communication is crucial for fostering trust, mitigating misinterpretations, and guaranteeing agreement between parents on significant issues concerning their children's development. Frequent communication channels, such as phone conversations, emails, or specialized co-parenting applications, offer a forum for talking about the kids' welfare, academic affairs, extracurricular pursuits, and other pertinent topics.

Effective co-parenting requires keeping personal feelings apart from the co-parenting dynamic. Even if you still carry feelings from a previous relationship, you must categorize them and put the kids' needs first. Co-parents can work together more skilfully and create a setting where kids feel safe and loved by both parents by keeping an eye on the shared responsibility of parenting. For co-parents who are facing emotional difficulties, getting professional help—such as counselling or therapy—can be helpful. It offers a haven to discuss persistent problems and create coping mechanisms.

Establishing a structured and consistent parenting plan is vital to effective co-parenting. A parenting plan outlines the agreed-upon schedule for the children, including visitation arrangements, holidays, and special occasions. Clarity and consistency in the parenting plan reduce uncertainty for parents and children, promoting stability. Flexibility is also essential, as unexpected events may require adjustments to the plan. Co-parents who demonstrate flexibility and a willingness to accommodate each other's schedules contribute to a more cooperative and less contentious co-parenting dynamic.

Respecting each other's parenting styles is another crucial element of effective co-parenting. Recognizing and accepting that co-parents may have different approaches to discipline, routines, and daily life is essential for creating a harmonious co-parenting environment. Children benefit when parents can maintain a united front on important issues while allowing room for individual parenting styles to coexist. Constructive discussions about parenting philosophies, expectations, and priorities can help align parenting strategies and minimize conflicts.

Encouraging and facilitating a positive relationship between the children and both parents is paramount in co-parenting. Children benefit significantly from having strong and supportive relationships with both parents, and co-parents play a crucial role in fostering these connections. Facilitating regular and meaningful visitation, encouraging open communication between children and the non-residential parent, and refraining from negative comments about the other parent contributes to a positive co-parenting atmosphere. Encouraging the kids' interactions with their extended family might help them feel even more connected and like they belong.

Flexibility and adaptability serve co-parents well in navigating the ever-changing landscape of co-parenting. Life circumstances, work schedules, and the children's needs may evolve, requiring co-parents to adapt their parenting plans and communication strategies accordingly. Co-parents willing to collaborate and adjust to changing circumstances create a resilient and responsive co-parenting dynamic.

Managing conflicts effectively is an inevitable aspect of co-parenting. Conflicts may occur, but how they are resolved will determine how they affect the co-parenting dynamic and, ultimately, the children. Empathy, active listening, and emphasis on finding solutions more than assigning blame are all components of healthy dispute resolution. Co-parents can acquire good communication and conflict resolution skills through co-parenting education programs, mediation, or therapy. Co-parents can create a more stable home atmosphere by modeling positive problem-solving for their kids and constructively resolving problems.

Consistency in shared values and expectations is crucial for children's well-being. Co-parents can collaborate on establishing consistent rules and expectations across both households, ensuring that the children experience continuity in their upbringing. Agreement on bedtime routines, homework expectations, and screen time rules helps create a seamless transition for the children between both homes. Consistency gives children a sense of security and predictability, contributing to their emotional well-being.

In cases where one co-parent faces significant life changes, such as relocation or remarriage, open communication and cooperation become even more critical. The impact of such changes on the children's lives should be discussed transparently between co-parents, and adjustments to the parenting plan may be necessary. Co-parents who prioritize the children's best interests and demonstrate flexibility during such transitions contribute to a more adaptive and supportive co-parenting environment.

The involvement of step-parents or new partners adds a layer to the co-parenting dynamic. Open communication and mutual respect between co-parents and step-parents are essential for creating a supportive and inclusive family structure. Co-parents should establish boundaries, roles, and expectations with step-parents while fostering positive relationships between step-parents and the children. Maintaining a united front and demonstrating respect for all parental figures in the children's lives contributes to a cohesive family unit.

Regular check-ins on the children's well-being, academic progress, and any concerns they may have to provide co-parents with valuable insights into their children's lives. Coordinating efforts to support the children's education, health, and extracurricular activities helps create a united front in addressing the children's needs. The shared responsibility for the children's overall well-being forms the foundation of effective co-parenting.

In conclusion, effective co-parenting is a continuous and intentional effort that requires communication, collaboration, and a commitment to the children's best interests. Navigating the complexities of co-parenting involves recognizing and managing personal emotions, establishing clear communication channels, and prioritizing consistency in parenting strategies. By fostering positive relationships with each other, respecting individual parenting styles, and adapting to changing circumstances, co-parents contribute to a stable and supportive environment for their children. Effective co-parenting lays the groundwork for the children to thrive emotionally, socially, and academically, setting the stage for a positive and resilient family dynamic.

Communication Between Parents

Communication between parents is a fundamental element that shapes the dynamics of a family. How parents communicate profoundly influences not only their relationship but also the well-being and development of their children. Effective communication fosters understanding, collaboration, and a sense of unity, creating a positive family environment. In this section, we explore the significance of communication between parents, the challenges it may entail, and strategies to enhance the quality of communication within a family setting.

Effective communication between parents begins with the cultivation of open and transparent dialogue. Establishing an environment where both parents feel comfortable expressing their thoughts, feelings, and concerns is crucial for building mutual understanding. Open communication lays the foundation for a partnership in which parents can collaboratively navigate the various aspects of family life, from parenting decisions to resolving conflicts. When parents communicate openly, they create a model for their children, teaching them the value of expressing themselves honestly and respectfully.

A vital element of parent-to-parent communication that works well is active listening. Respect and a sense of validation are fostered when people listen intently to one another's viewpoints without interjecting or providing answers right away. Hearing what is being said and comprehending the underlying feelings and intentions are both components of active listening. Parents who actively listen to their children show empathy and foster an environment where all parents are respected and heard.

Building a solid family unit requires open and constant communication. To prevent misconceptions, parents should try to communicate their expectations, values, and parenting techniques clearly and concisely. When communication within the family is consistent, it helps establish predictability, which enables kids to comprehend the standards and expectations of the family. Clear and consistent communication between parents and children creates a stable, safe atmosphere that benefits the children's emotional health.

Effective communication is not solely about expressing thoughts and feelings but also about choosing the right timing and context for discussions. Understanding when to have meaningful conversations and creating a conducive environment for communication contributes to the overall effectiveness of the interaction. Parents can benefit from choosing appropriate discussion times, ensuring minimal distractions and a relaxed atmosphere that encourages open dialogue.

Parents must be aware of their nonverbal cues because they can improve or impair spoken communication. Maintaining eye contact, nodding, and adopting open postures are examples of positive body language that help foster understanding and a sense of connection between parents.

Differing communication styles, personal stressors, or unsolved issues are common causes of communication challenges between parents. Acknowledging and tackling these obstacles is imperative to preserve a positive family dynamic. Parents who communicate differently from one another can establish areas of agreement and modify their methods to suit one another better. It is important to encourage each other during difficult moments since parents may unwittingly reflect their anger onto each other during stressful situations. Unresolved disputes can effectively impede communication. Therefore, parents should actively work to address them through direct discussion, compromise, and, if needed, outside help.

The role of emotional intelligence in communication between parents is paramount. Emotional intelligence involves recognizing and understanding one's emotions and those of others. Parents with high emotional intelligence can navigate conversations with empathy, manage conflicts constructively, and adapt their communication style to different situations. Cultivating emotional intelligence is a continuous process that enhances the quality of interpersonal relationships within the family.

Constructive conflict resolution is an integral aspect of effective communication between parents. Disagreements are natural in any relationship, but how conflicts are handled significantly impacts the family dynamic. Healthy conflict resolution involves respecting, focusing on the specific issue, and seeking mutually beneficial solutions. Learning and using conflict resolution techniques like compromise, active listening, and finding common ground can benefit parents.

Parental teamwork is a decisive outcome of effective communication. When parents view themselves as a team working towards providing a nurturing and supportive environment for their children, the family dynamic is strengthened. Teamwork involves shared decision-making, collaborative problem-solving, and a sense of unity in facing the challenges of parenthood. Parents who perceive themselves as a team model positive behavior for their children and contribute to a harmonious family atmosphere.

The impact of communication between parents extends beyond the parental relationship to influence the overall family culture. Positive communication patterns contribute to developing a healthy family culture characterized by trust, cooperation, and a shared sense of purpose. In contrast, ineffective communication can contribute to a hostile family culture marked by tension, miscommunication, and an overall lack of cohesion. Parents have the opportunity to shape the family culture through intentional and positive communication practices.

Incorporating family meetings into the routine can enhance communication and collaboration between parents. Regular family meetings provide a structured space for discussing upcoming events, addressing concerns, and involving children in decision-making when appropriate. Family meetings promote a sense of inclusivity and create a forum for open communication, fostering a family environment where everyone feels valued and heard.

Parental role models significantly impact children's interpersonal relationships and communication skills. Youngsters pick up communication skills from watching their parents argue and agree. Parents who demonstrate practical communication skills, including active listening, empathy, and constructive conflict resolution, provide their children with a valuable blueprint for healthy relationships. Conversely, parents who engage in ineffective communication may inadvertently pass on negative communication patterns to their children.

Technology has become integral to modern communication, and its impact on family dynamics cannot be overlooked. While technology offers convenience, it can also contribute to challenges such as decreased face-to-face interaction, miscommunication through text messages, and the potential for distractions during family time. Parents should be mindful of their technology use and strive to create a balance that allows for meaningful in-person communication and connection within the family.

In conclusion, communication between parents is the cornerstone of a healthy family dynamic. Open and transparent dialogue, active listening, and consistent communication contribute to understanding, collaboration, and a positive family culture. Challenges in communication can be addressed by recognizing and addressing differing communication styles, fostering emotional intelligence, and practicing constructive conflict resolution. The way parents communicate not only influences their relationship but also shapes the overall family environment, impacting the well-being and development of their children. By prioritizing effective communication, parents contribute to a family dynamic characterized by trust, unity, and a shared commitment to nurturing a supportive and loving home.

Balancing Responsibilities

In the intricate dance of modern life, individuals are often confronted with many responsibilities, ranging from personal commitments to professional obligations. Achieving a delicate balance among these various responsibilities is an ongoing challenge that requires strategic planning, adaptability, and a keen understanding of personal priorities. This section delves into the complexities of balancing responsibilities, exploring the impact on individuals' well-being, the challenges posed by competing demands, and strategies for achieving a harmonious equilibrium in pursuing a fulfilling and meaningful life.

The contemporary landscape is characterized by an ever-increasing array of responsibilities that individuals must juggle. The sheer amount of responsibilities—ranging from the demands of a busy career to duties to family, friends, and personal interests—can be debilitating. In pursuing a successful and fulfilling life, individuals often navigate a delicate balancing act, where allocating time, energy, and attention becomes a critical determinant of overall well-being.

One of the primary challenges in balancing responsibilities is the potential for competing demands to create stress and feelings of being overwhelmed. The pressures of meeting deadlines at work, attending to familial responsibilities, and nurturing personal relationships can create a sense of perpetual urgency. If this high-stress level is not managed, it may harm an individual's physical and emotional well-being. To mitigate the negative consequences of stress, preserving the delicate equilibrium required for effective responsibility management becomes critical.

Career-related responsibilities often occupy a significant portion of an individual's time and energy. The demands of a fast-paced and competitive professional environment can lead to long working hours, tight deadlines, and the constant pursuit of career advancement. While career success is a meaningful pursuit, an imbalance that prioritizes work over personal well-being can result in burnout, diminished job satisfaction, and strained relationships. A harmonious balance between professional ambitions and personal fulfillment is essential for sustained career growth and overall life satisfaction.

Family responsibilities, including parenting, caring for aging parents, and maintaining a household, present another layer of complexity in the balancing act of modern life. The expectations and demands associated with familial roles can be both rewarding and challenging. Balancing the needs of family members while tending to one's personal growth and aspirations requires a nuanced approach. The ability to navigate these family responsibilities flexibly and effectively manage time is crucial for fostering a supportive and harmonious family environment.

Social and community responsibilities add dimension to individuals' intricate tapestry of obligations. Engaging in social activities, volunteering, or contributing to community initiatives enriches one's sense of connection and purpose. However, finding the right balance between social commitments and personal time is essential. Overcommitment to social responsibilities can lead to exhaustion and detract from basic self-care practices, ultimately impacting overall well-being.

In the pursuit of balancing responsibilities, personal well-being should not be sacrificed. Self-care, encompassing physical, emotional, and mental well-being, is a foundational element that contributes to an individual's ability to navigate life's complexities. Refraining from neglecting self-care in the pursuit of fulfilling responsibilities can result in burnout, fatigue, and a diminished capacity to meet obligations effectively. Maintaining resilience and general happiness requires acknowledging the significance of self-care and incorporating it into the overall strategy for managing responsibilities.

Even if technology provides never-before-seen connectedness and ease, it is harder to balance obligations. The continual barrage of emails, texts, and alerts can lead to a persistent feeling of being "on call," making it harder to distinguish between personal and professional life. Setting limits, setting priorities, and developing a positive connection with technology are all necessary for effective time management in the digital age to keep it from being a stressor rather than an efficiency aid.

Strategies for balancing responsibilities encompass a multifaceted approach considering individual priorities, effective time management, and cultivating resilience. Setting priorities is essential; people must recognize and concentrate on duties and obligations consistent with their core beliefs and long-term objectives. This intentional strategy aids people in devoting their time and effort to pursuits with the most significant potential to improve their happiness and sense of fulfillment.

Implementing techniques like making timetables, establishing reasonable deadlines, and using productivity tools are all part of effective time management. Making obligations more realistic and lowering the chance of feeling overwhelmed can be achieved by breaking extensive activities into more minor, more manageable phases. Moreover, when feasible, embracing the power of delegation allows individuals to share responsibilities and lighten their load, fostering a more collaborative approach to managing obligations.

Flexibility is an essential quality in the pursuit of balancing responsibilities. Life is dynamic, and unforeseen challenges or opportunities may arise. Individuals who approach their responsibilities with adaptability and a willingness to adjust their plans when necessary are better equipped to navigate the complexities of modern life. Resilience, or the capacity to pick oneself up after failure, is essential for preserving composure in the face of unforeseen difficulties.

Effective communication within personal and professional relationships is a cornerstone of successfully managing responsibilities. Clear and open communication allows individuals to express their needs, establish expectations, and negotiate shared responsibilities collaboratively. In familial and social contexts, communication helps create a mutual understanding of priorities and encourages a supportive network that facilitates balancing.

Establishing boundaries is a vital component of achieving a balance among responsibilities. Clear delineation between work and personal life, defining limits on social commitments, and setting realistic expectations for oneself contribute to a more sustainable approach to responsibility management. Boundaries create space for individuals to engage in self-care, pursue personal interests, and recharge, ultimately enhancing their ability to meet obligations effectively.

Mindfulness practices, such as meditation and reflection, offer valuable tools for individuals striving to balance responsibilities. Through the cultivation of a heightened awareness of the present moment, these activities enable people to approach their obligations with intentionality and attention. Additionally, mindfulness can be used as a coping strategy to control stress and lessen the damaging effects of conflicting demands on mental health.

In summary, juggling obligations in the modern world is a dynamic and complex task that calls for deliberate effort and a calculated strategy. Setting priorities, using time wisely, and being resilient is essential for juggling the demands of a job, family, social life, and personal commitments. Maintaining a harmonious balance is crucial for emotional wellbeing and helps build a purposeful and happy existence. Through deliberate tactics, encouraging flexibility, and appreciating the value of self-care, people can successfully manage the complex dance of obligations and have meaningful lives.

CHAPTER X

Addressing Specific Parental Challenges

Dealing with Teenage Rebellion

The journey through adolescence is marked by a myriad of physical and psychological transformations as teenagers navigate the path to self-discovery and independence. During this phase, parents often face the challenges of teenage rebellion—a complex and usually tumultuous period where teenagers assert their autonomy and challenge established authority figures. This section delves into the intricacies of dealing with teenage rebellion, exploring the underlying causes, the impact on parent-teen relationships, and strategies for fostering understanding and communication during this crucial developmental stage.

Teenage rebellion is a natural and expected aspect of adolescent development, rooted in the teenager's quest for autonomy and a distinct identity. As teenagers undergo profound physical, emotional, and cognitive changes, they grapple with the desire to establish their individuality, separate from parental influence. This quest for independence often manifests as rebellion against rules, questioning authority, and exploring new ideas and experiences. Even though teenage rebellion is a standard part of growing up, keeping a positive and healthy parent-teen connection depends on recognizing its causes and overcoming its obstacles.

One of the primary drivers of teenage rebellion is the desire for autonomy and a sense of control over one's life. As teenagers strive to define themselves independently of their parents, they may challenge rules and boundaries to assert their individuality. This process is essential for developing a strong and resilient sense of self. However, the clash between a teenager's desire for autonomy and a parent's responsibility for their well-being can create tension within the family dynamic.

Communication breakdown is a common challenge during periods of teenage rebellion. Teenagers may feel misunderstood or unfairly restricted, leading to a breakdown in effective communication with their parents. The generation gap, differing perspectives, and the emotional intensity of adolescence further contribute to this breakdown. Parents must recognize the importance of maintaining open lines of communication, even in the face of rebellion, to foster mutual understanding and navigate the challenges posed by this developmental phase.

Peer influence plays a significant role in teenage rebellion. As teenagers seek to establish their identity, peer relationships become paramount. Teenagers may adopt behaviors directly at odds with their parents' expectations and ideals due to peer pressure and the need to fit in. Adolescents' rebellious dynamics are influenced by the tension that results from opposing pressures, such as peer pressure and parental guidance.

Parents often struggle to distinguish between everyday teenage rebellion and more concerning behaviors that may warrant intervention. Experimentation with identity, values, and interests is a natural part of adolescence. However, behaviors that pose risks to the teenager's well-being, such as substance abuse, involvement in risky activities, or severe academic decline, may signal underlying issues that require parental attention. Differentiating between typical rebellious behavior and potential red flags requires careful observation and an awareness of the teenager's baseline behaviors.

Strategies for dealing with teenage rebellion center around fostering open communication, understanding the underlying motivations, and establishing a foundation of mutual respect. A vital element of communicating effectively with teenagers is active listening. An environment that makes teenagers feel acknowledged and heard promotes more candid conversations. In addition to expressing concern for their well-being, parents should comprehend the teen's point of view and respect their need for independence.

Managing teenage rebellion requires establishing limits that are constant and unambiguous. Teens want autonomy, but to successfully negotiate the challenges of puberty, they also need structure and direction. Teens have a framework in which to exercise their freedom responsibly when there are clear expectations and norms in place. Encouraging teens to negotiate rules, giving them a say in decisions, and instilling a feeling of accountability for their behavior are crucial.

In times of rebellion, a positive parent-teen relationship is built on mutual respect. A teen's sense of agency and self-worth is enhanced when their demand for independence is acknowledged and respected, even when it goes against what their parents would want. Similarly, parents should be respected for their roles as decision-makers and caregivers. Finding a balance between individuality and deference to authority promotes a less aggressive and cooperative dynamic.

Empathy is a powerful tool for parents navigating teenage rebellion. Recognizing adolescence's challenges and emotional intensity allows parents to approach conflicts with understanding and compassion. While setting boundaries is essential, approaching rule enforcement with empathy helps teenagers feel acknowledged and supported. Empathetic communication fosters a sense of connection and promotes the development of a secure attachment between parents and teenagers.

Encouraging open discussions about values, expectations, and consequences helps teenagers internalize the reasoning behind rules. Explaining the rationale behind decisions, rather than relying solely on directives, fosters critical thinking and a deeper understanding of the principles guiding parental choices. This approach encourages teenagers to develop their internal compass and make informed decisions based on shared family values.

Addressing Specific Parental Challenges

Using positive reinforcement to mold behavior is quite effective during teenage rebellion. Recognizing and praising positive behaviors reinforces the teenager's sense of accomplishment and fosters a positive parent-teen relationship. Positive reinforcement can take various forms, from verbal encouragement to acknowledging achievements and fostering a supportive environment that encourages positive choices.

Maintaining a supportive and non-judgmental stance is crucial when dealing with teenage rebellion. Teenagers may hesitate to share their thoughts and experiences if they fear harsh judgment or punishment. Creating an environment where teenagers feel safe expressing themselves without fear of immediate repercussions fosters trust and encourages honest communication. A supportive stance does not imply condoning inappropriate behavior but demonstrates a commitment to understanding and guiding the teenager through challenges.

Seeking professional support may be necessary in cases where teenage rebellion escalates to concerning behaviors or significantly impacts the teenager's well-being. Therapeutic intervention provides a neutral and constructive space for both parents and teenagers to explore underlying issues, improve communication, and develop strategies for navigating the challenges of adolescence. Professional guidance can foster positive change and strengthen the parent-child relationship.

In conclusion, dealing with teenage rebellion is a nuanced and multifaceted process that requires empathy, effective communication, and a commitment to mutual respect. Recognizing the underlying motivations behind rebellion, fostering open dialogue, and setting clear boundaries contribute to a healthier parent-teen relationship. While teenage rebellion is a normal part of adolescent development, navigating it with sensitivity and understanding lays the groundwork for the teenager's successful transition to independence and adulthood. Through intentional efforts to maintain connection and support, parents can guide their teenagers through the tumultuous waters of rebellion, fostering growth, resilience, and a strong foundation for future relationships.

Handling Sibling Conflicts

Within the intricate tapestry of family dynamics, sibling relationships are a unique and complex thread that weaves through the fabric of our lives. While these relationships can be a source of companionship, support, and lifelong friendship, they also carry the potential for conflicts that arise from shared living spaces, differing personalities, and the natural competition inherent in sibling bonds. This section explores the nuances of handling sibling conflicts, delving into the factors contributing to disagreements, the impact on family dynamics, and practical strategies for fostering harmony and understanding among siblings.

Sibling conflicts are an inherent aspect of family life, emerging from sibling relationships' close and often intense nature. The shared history, everyday experiences, and proximity in age create a fertile ground for camaraderie and discord. Conflicts may arise from various sources, including differences in personality, varying interests, and the natural desire for autonomy and individuality. Understanding the multifaceted nature of sibling conflicts is crucial for parents and caregivers seeking to navigate these challenges and promote positive sibling relationships.

One of the primary contributors to sibling conflicts is the competition for parental attention and resources. Siblings may vie for recognition, approval, or affection from parents, leading to feelings of rivalry and jealousy. Birth order can also significantly shape sibling dynamics, with firstborns often assuming leadership roles and younger siblings seeking ways to assert themselves. Parents who want to establish an environment where each sibling feels appreciated and supported must acknowledge and deal with these relationships.

Differing personalities and interests among siblings can contribute to conflicts as they navigate shared spaces and resources within the family. Siblings may have distinct preferences, hobbies, or temperaments that clash, leading to disagreements over how shared spaces are used or how common resources are allocated. Acknowledging and respecting these differences is vital for creating an inclusive family environment that celebrates each sibling's individuality while fostering cooperation.

Parental influence on sibling conflicts cannot be understated. How parents model conflict resolution, communication, and the expression of emotions significantly shapes how siblings handle disagreements. Parents who provide a healthy model for resolving conflicts through effective communication, compromise, and empathy contribute to developing positive conflict resolution skills among their children. Conversely, parents who model unhealthy conflict behaviors may inadvertently contribute to escalating sibling conflicts.

The impact of sibling conflicts extends beyond the immediate participants, influencing the overall family dynamic. Persistent and unresolved conflicts can create tension, stress, and a sense of unease within the family. Siblings may feel compelled to take sides or seek alliances, further exacerbating the divide. The emotional toll of ongoing conflicts can strain parent-child relationships and disrupt the family's unity. Addressing sibling conflicts proactively is essential for maintaining a positive family atmosphere.

Practical strategies for handling sibling conflicts revolve around fostering communication, teaching conflict resolution skills, and promoting empathy within the family. Open communication is a cornerstone for resolving disputes among siblings. Parents must establish a safe space where kids may freely express their thoughts, feelings, and opinions without worrying about being judged. Encouraging siblings to communicate directly with each other rather than through parents promotes autonomy and personal responsibility in resolving conflicts.

Teaching conflict resolution skills equips siblings with the tools to navigate disagreements constructively. Strategies such as active listening, expressing feelings using "I" statements, and finding compromise empower siblings to work together in finding mutually acceptable solutions. Parents can actively facilitate these skills by guiding siblings through the resolution process, offering suggestions for compromise, and reinforcing positive communication patterns.

Promoting empathy within the family is a powerful antidote to sibling conflicts. Encouraging siblings to consider each other's perspectives, feelings, and needs fosters a deeper understanding and connection. Parents can engage in activities that cultivate empathy, such as discussing the impact of actions on others, encouraging siblings to walk in each other's shoes, and emphasizing the importance of mutual support and kindness. Empathy is a foundation for building positive sibling relationships based on understanding and compassion.

Establishing clear and consistent family rules and expectations helps mitigate potential sources of conflict. Conflicts are less likely to arise when siblings have a shared understanding of acceptable behaviors, responsibilities, and boundaries. Consistency in enforcing rules ensures that all siblings are held to the same standards, fostering a sense of fairness and equality within the family. Clear expectations contribute to a harmonious family environment where members understand their roles and responsibilities.

Creating opportunities for positive sibling interactions is essential for strengthening sibling bonds and reducing conflicts. Family activities, shared hobbies, and collaborative projects allow siblings to connect, collaborate, and appreciate each other's strengths. These positive interactions build a foundation of mutual respect and shared experiences, contributing to the overall resilience of sibling relationships. Parents can play an active role in facilitating these opportunities, fostering a sense of camaraderie among siblings.

Encouraging siblings to take ownership of their conflicts and find solutions promotes autonomy and personal responsibility. While parental guidance and intervention may sometimes be necessary, empowering siblings to resolve disputes fosters independence and conflict-resolution skills. This approach contributes to developing a collaborative mindset, where siblings learn to navigate conflicts together rather than relying solely on parental intervention.

Establishing designated spaces for each sibling within the home helps mitigate conflicts over territory and personal belongings. Whether through shared bedrooms, designated study spaces, or other living areas, providing siblings with a sense of ownership and personal space reduces the likelihood of disagreements over boundaries. Respect for personal space contributes to a more harmonious coexistence, where each sibling feels a sense of autonomy and control within the family environment.

Parents must remain mindful of favoritism, as perceived or fundamental imbalances in attention or treatment can fuel sibling conflicts. While it is natural for parents to have different relationships with each child based on personality and shared interests, efforts should ensure that all siblings feel equally valued and supported. Addressing concerns of favoritism directly and celebrating each child's unique qualities can help mitigate feelings of resentment and competition.

In cases where conflicts persist or escalate, seeking professional guidance may be beneficial. Family therapists or counselors can provide valuable insights into underlying dynamics, offer conflict resolution strategies, and facilitate family communication. Professional support is crucial when conflicts contribute to significant distress or strain the family dynamic.

In conclusion, handling sibling conflicts requires a nuanced and proactive approach that focuses on communication, conflict resolution skills, and fostering positive relationships within the family. Understanding the sources of disputes, addressing them proactively, and promoting empathy and mutual respect contribute to a harmonious sibling dynamic. While conflicts are inevitable in sibling relationships, they also present opportunities for growth, understanding, and developing crucial life skills. Through intentional efforts to create a supportive family environment, parents can nurture positive sibling relationships that endure beyond childhood, enriching the lives of each family member.

Navigating Special Parenting Situations (e.g., Single Parenting)

Parenting is a dynamic journey that unfolds uniquely for each family, and within this diverse landscape, certain circumstances present distinctive challenges. Special parenting situations, such as single parenting, demand resilience, adaptability, and a tailored approach to address the unique needs of parents and children. This section explores the complexities of navigating special parenting situations, delving into the challenges single parents face and other unique family structures while examining effective strategies for fostering a nurturing and supportive environment.

Single parenting, in particular, is a parenting situation that comes with its own set of challenges. The role of a single parent involves shouldering the responsibilities traditionally divided between two parents, including financial support, emotional nurturing, and day-to-day caregiving. The absence of a co-parent can contribute to feelings of isolation and heightened stress, as single parents often grapple with the demands of raising children while managing their own well-being and career responsibilities.

One of the primary challenges single parents' faces is the need to balance multiple roles without the support of a partner. Juggling work commitments, household responsibilities, and the emotional needs of children can be overwhelming. Single parents often navigate a delicate equilibrium, seeking stability and support while facing the inevitable constraints of time and resources. Recognizing the unique demands of single parenting is crucial for developing strategies that promote both parental and child well-being.

Financial strain is another significant challenge faced by many single parents. The absence of a second income can place single-parent households at a higher risk of economic instability. Meeting children's basic needs, such as housing, education, and healthcare, may require careful budgeting and resourcefulness. Single parents may also encounter difficulties securing affordable and reliable childcare, contributing to financial stability issues.

Addressing Specific Parental Challenges

The emotional toll of single parenting is considerable. Single parents may experience feelings of loneliness, exhaustion, and self-doubt as they navigate the complexities of parenthood without a partner. To overcome these obstacles, single parents may find it helpful to establish a robust support system of friends, family, and local services. Making contact with other single parents can create a sense of solidarity by offering a platform for sharing thoughts and experiences.

Effective time management is paramount for single parents, given the myriad responsibilities they must handle independently. Balancing work commitments, household chores, and quality time with children requires strategic planning and prioritization. Single parents may find it helpful to create a realistic schedule that allocates time for work, self-care, and dedicated moments with their children. Flexibility and adaptability are key as unexpected challenges may arise, necessitating adjustments to the daily routine.

Co-parenting arrangements, where both parents share responsibilities despite living separately, represent another unique parenting situation. While co-parenting offers the potential for shared caregiving responsibilities, effective communication and collaboration between parents are crucial. Establishing clear boundaries, expectations, and a consistent parenting approach contributes to a stable and supportive environment for children. Co-parents should prioritize open communication, maintain flexibility, and prioritize the child's well-being above personal conflicts.

Blended families, formed when parents with children from previous relationships come together, present another set of challenges. The dynamics of blending different family structures require sensitivity, understanding, and a commitment to fostering a harmonious environment. Children in blended families may need time to adjust to new family members and roles. Clear communication, establishing shared values, and creating opportunities for bonding can contribute to the successful integration of family members in a blended setting.

Children with special needs require specialized parenting approaches, and parents in these situations must navigate unique challenges associated with healthcare, education, and emotional support. Advocating for the specific needs of a child with disabilities or special needs demands resilience and a commitment to ensuring access to appropriate resources and accommodations. Building a solid support network, including professionals, support groups, and educators, can be instrumental in navigating the complexities of parenting a child with special needs.

Strategies for navigating special parenting situations revolve around building a solid support network, accessing available resources, and prioritizing self-care. Single parents, for instance, can benefit from seeking assistance from family and friends, utilizing community resources, and exploring support groups where they can connect with others facing similar challenges. Financial assistance programs, childcare services, and educational support can also alleviate some of the burdens of single parenting.

Addressing Specific Parental Challenges

Effective communication is essential in any particular parenting situation. Whether separated or forming a blended family, co-parents must prioritize open and honest communication to navigate shared responsibilities and address potential conflicts. Families dealing with particular difficulties may find it especially helpful to seek professional assistance, such as family therapy or counseling, which offers a haven for discussing issues and creating productive communication plans.

Education and empowerment play a pivotal role in navigating special parenting situations. Single parents, co-parents, and those in blended families can benefit from seeking information and resources catering to their specific needs. Understanding legal rights, accessing parenting resources, and staying informed about available support services contribute to a parent's ability to navigate challenges effectively. Empowering parents with knowledge and skills enhances their capacity to make informed decisions that align with the best interests of their children.

Self-care is a fundamental aspect of navigating special parenting situations. Whether managing the demands of single parenting, co-parenting, or raising children with special needs, parents must prioritize their well-being to support their children effectively. This entails scheduling downtime for leisure, pursuing hobbies, and getting emotional support as required. A parent's ability to maintain their physical and mental health directly impacts their capacity to meet the unique challenges of their parenting situation.

Flexibility and adaptability are inherent to successful parenting in any unique situation. Recognizing that challenges may arise unexpectedly allows parents to approach their roles resiliently. Embracing flexibility in parenting styles, routines, and expectations fosters an environment where both parents and children can navigate the complexities of their situation with greater ease. The ability to adapt to changing circumstances contributes to a positive and supportive family environment.

In conclusion, navigating special parenting situations requires a combination of resilience, resourcefulness, and a commitment to fostering a nurturing environment. Single parents, co-parents, and those in blended or blended families face distinct challenges that demand tailored strategies and support. Prioritizing effective communication, seeking available resources, and embracing flexibility contribute to successfully navigating these unique parenting dynamics. Empowering parents with knowledge, building strong support networks, and prioritizing self-care creates a foundation for fostering positive parent-child relationships, regardless of the specific challenges presented by each family's unique circumstances.

CONCLUSION

In conclusion, "Calm Parenting: A Guide to Anger Management for Moms and Dads - Nurturing Harmony amid Parenthood" seeks to empower parents with valuable insights and practical strategies for maintaining composure and fostering a harmonious atmosphere within the family. Parenthood is undoubtedly a challenging journey, and the book acknowledges the inevitable stressors that can trigger anger and frustration. By delving into the origins of parental outrage, exploring its impact on parent-child relationships, and providing a comprehensive set of tools for managing and preventing anger, the e-book strives to offer a holistic approach to emotional well-being for both parents and children.

Throughout the e-book, readers are encouraged to recognize the emotional triggers contributing to anger, understanding that self-awareness is a fundamental step towards positive change. The importance of effective communication, stress management techniques, and mindfulness in parenting is emphasized, providing parents with practical methods to navigate the complex emotions that arise while raising children.

Moreover, the e-book underscores the significance of parental self-care, acknowledging that maintaining one's emotional balance is integral to providing a nurturing and supportive environment for children. By addressing parenting challenges with empathy, assertive communication, and a focus on positive reinforcement, the e-book aims to guide parents toward a more mindful and calm approach to their roles.

As parents navigate the intricacies of raising children, the book is a companion, offering valuable insights and actionable strategies to promote a healthier and more harmonious family dynamic. By fostering understanding, empathy, and effective communication, "Calm Parenting" aspires to create an environment where both parents and children can thrive emotionally, forging lasting bonds built on trust, love, and mutual respect.

Thank you for buying and reading/listening to our book. If you found this book useful/helpful please take a few minutes and leave a review on the platform where you purchased our book. Your feedback matters greatly to us.

www.ingramcontent.com/pod-product-compliance
Lightning Source LLC
LaVergne TN
LVHW012022060526
838201LV00061B/4415